CW01511842

Unstoppable by Design

Real Life Stories of ADHD, Grit and Success

Authors

Dr Phil Anderton

Natasha Davies

Francesca James

John Reynolds

Editors

Kevin Thistlethwaite & Linda Goodman

Design

Tom Sullivan

Print

Advanced Print Services

Contents

UNSTOPPABLE BY DESIGN

ABOUT THE COVER

I was sat at a Christmas table with my extended family all around me when my sister in law's father, the art legend Leonard Creo, 'Creo', who was then over 90 years of age, sat with me. A gentle, engaging gentleman, he asked me to participate in an experiment with him. *"Indulge me"* he said. These are my recollections of that conversation:

Creo set out over a dozen original art prints in front of me. Each 7x5 and slightly different. *"Choose your favourite half a dozen"* he said, *"choose what you like, you, your choice"*. Having done so he quizzed me on why I had made those choices. The colours, the way the prints captured energy, struggle, success, those chosen by me illustrated those emotions in me, coming from his original artwork, more than those discarded.

"Fabulous, art is about emotion and you have got just what I was looking for when I created these pictures, now shorten the list to just two". Having complied, he again engaged me in discussion. *"My art has always had a purpose Phil, always. It's never been a job, it is a passion and a calling. Now choose the picture that best captures your emotions"*. Believing I was now assisting him in a meaningful experiment and an exercise to allow him to explain the purpose of Art to me, I pondered and made my choice. This one I exclaimed, yes, this one.

"Does that capture, more than the others, look back at them, check, does this artwork capture those emotions you said came from the pictures when you first saw them?". I confirmed they did.

"Do you remember how you used one of my pictures for the cover of your first book? I am proud you did that. I am sure I and many of my family have this ADHD you work with. And to have the cover of the book you wrote as one of my pictures is what Art is all about."

"If you don't mind, I would ask that you use this picture for your next book. You talk about people with ADHD climbing up their own ladder, of achieving new heights when they understand, and how they can be inspired into success by a diagnosis and maybe treatment. You have described to me the emotions of 'energy' 'struggle' ,'colour' and 'success' as you see in this picture. You have chosen the cover of your next book".

Creo has long since passed and his memory, through his Art and family leadership, lives on. Like any many great and acclaimed artists, I am convinced he was neurodivergent and probably ADHD. Some of his children are, proudly.

The full circle impact of that event for me cannot be understated. I hope you 'get it' and enjoy the world-class Art of a truly great man.

*Dr Phil Anderton
Author, father, and stepfather to an amazing neurodivergent son, employer of many proud neurodivergent team members and a man on a mission.

Foreword

In 2002, when I first started working with ADHD, many didn't understand the implications and impact of having ADHD. In those days, adult ADHD had not been recognised, and young girls were merely thought of as dreamers in the back of a classroom. ADHD was a naughty boy thing.

Thankfully, that landscape of understanding has changed significantly and both adults and all genders are now fully recognised.

In 2019, when we started ADHD 360, with the goal of becoming a world-class ADHD and then Autism service, my co-founders and I knew we had a battle. To progress service standards, to embrace science and to follow our hearts was placing us firmly in the descriptive bracket of 'disrupters'. The established providers did not welcome us. However, fast forward and now ADHD 360 provides licensed services to the NHS and is a force to be reckoned with. Even those words and that story will, I suggest, resonate with any entrepreneur reading this book.

In 2003, I was given the incredible opportunity to review Wilbur and Orville Wright, the Wright Brothers, school reports. Both were described as mischievous and neither graduated from their mid-west public school. Grades were, at best, described as mediocre, except for science and both were reported to have 'lost interest in school at an early age'. Both were described as not engaging and not achieving their potential. Fascinated by mechanics and encouraged by their father, they opened a bicycle repair shop as young teenagers alongside their already established printing business. Their father was described as obstinate, driven, and stubborn, who took risks to join the great American Gold Rush in 1854 despite being an ordained priest. Even then, the hereditary nature of ADHD-like behaviours were evident, from father to sons.

Over time, their 'hyperfocus' on aviation and aeronautics grew. The wayward brothers dedicated 13 years of their lives on that 'hyperfocus' passion and in 1903, they, of course, achieved the world's first powered flight. I am convinced that the brothers who changed the world were neurodivergent, probably ADHD and of course, they became revolutionary, visionary entrepreneurs.

Am I an entrepreneur? I doubt it. I had a concept of building the best service in the world for ADHD and relentlessly, I have pursued that goal. At the time of this book's conception, this has led to probably the world's largest service, with over 3,000 new patient assessments a month, as well as providing meaningful employment for over 400 bright, enthusiastic, and often 'neurospicy' workforce. My work family. We embrace tech, challenge the norm, and have designed and built a process-led, virtual neurodivergence hospital.

Fast-forward to 2024, when John Reynolds and I met at Ideas Fest (AKA Glastonbury for Business) in Tring, Hertfordshire in the UK. An immediate meeting of minds led to in-depth discussions about the whole ADHD 'movement' and the need for something to be available, publicly, that helped to 'remove the shame and change the narrative' for people with ADHD. Already a TV broadcaster, with a reputation for excellence, John and I formed the idea of the 'ADHD Beyond the Label' TV series and a new approach was born.

Extending invitations out to John's extensive contacts, we soon found ourselves in the TV studio with the most amazing people.

All our interviewees, partners on our journey now, have a back story of challenge, hardship and latterly for most, some success. What John and I soon realised, especially when discussing related matters with Francesca James (Frankie), is that many entrepreneurs are likely to have ADHD.

When analysed it stands to reason:

Why persist in conforming to fit in when your mind is making that tricky every day?

Is it not easier to follow a dream if you're slightly impulsive and make things happen?

If you have an innate ability to focus on one thing at a time, at the possible expense of everything else, why not do that?

And why not build a business concept using those skills?

The correlation between being an entrepreneur and having a neurodivergent approach to life are endless. And as they are endless, they are exciting.

Whilst it is important to validate the ADHD diagnosis by reviewing deficits, symptoms, and impairment, it is also relevant to celebrate success, achievement, and to ensure that we all FULLY understand ADHD from every available angle.

This book, a concept designed from a single conversation between John, Frankie and myself, aims to place a new set of foundations in the understanding of ADHD, particularly recognising how being an entrepreneur with ADHD is commonplace, a potential key to success, yet still an incredible struggle. We've also sought the perspectives and insights from those closest to our contributors, capturing their perspective on what it's like to live with and be around an ADHD entrepreneur. It is a fascinating and illuminative set of perspectives and as such, we continue to remove the shame and change the narrative.

An entrepreneur can be described as "an individual who creates a new business, bearing most of the risks and enjoying most of the rewards."

Creativity, a key trait of having ADHD, often drives people to create, sometimes from a mild impulse. Taking risks is another very common trait, as is seeking rewards, which can help feelings of past or present rejection and are an important element for success. Even by definition, therefore, entrepreneurial skills match the ADHD diagnostic criteria.

Recently, I was told by a Beyond the Label interviewee that 'everything is impossible until someone does it'. Orville Wright is quoted as stating, "Flight was looked upon as an impossibility."

I remain proud to work in the ADHD and Autism 'space' where perhaps nothing is impossible. I am surrounded by amazing people who get things done and despite each and every contributor's backstory captured in this book, at best, hardship is overcome and at worst, we work together to change the narrative, to achieve more and to be understood.

I am indebted to John Reynolds for the passion, companionship, and smiles, he is infectiously positive. To Michael Hammond for the incredible production and direction skills for Beyond the Label, to Frankie James for, well, for being the powerhouse that is Frankie. Natasha Davies, herself neurodivergent, has brought the concept of this book to life and interviewed the amazing contributors who make this so real. Her passion is unparalleled.

Finally, on behalf of John and myself, we would both like to sincerely thank our partners, Lesley (John's wife) and Samantha (my long-suffering wife), for their forbearance as we continue to work on the activity that hopefully is and will continue to make a small difference in the world of neurodivergence.

To our contributors, you are special, part of a new ecosystem of change and greater understanding and we hope that this publication helps you to recognise how amazing you are.

Dr Phil Anderton
CEO at ADHD360

UNSTOPPABLE BY DESIGN

The Story behind the Stories

"If you are always trying to be normal, you will never know how amazing you can be."

MAYA ANGELOU

From the moment we're old enough to understand 'the rules', many of us are taught that success comes from fitting in. Keep your head down. Don't make waves. Blend in. Tone it down. Follow the rules.

But for many of the people in this book, following the rules and the traditional expected life path was never an option. As their stories show, that's exactly why they've succeeded.

The idea for Beyond the ADHD Label was born from a conversation between Dr Phil Anderton, John Reynolds and Francesca James at Ideas Fest 2024. What began as a concept for a TV series, Beyond the ADHD Label, evolved into something bigger: a chance to capture, in print, the grit, determination, and unfiltered reality of entrepreneurs and innovators who are not just living with ADHD, but thriving because of it.

Every single contributor in these pages is living proof that the old story about ADHD is wrong. The stigma must go. These are people who have built their success not in spite of their ADHD, but often because of it.

The tired stereotype of the 'naughty little schoolboy who can't sit still' has no place here. ADHD is far more complex, far more human and as these stories show, far more powerful. Many of the voices you'll hear belong to adults diagnosed late in life, after decades of masking and trying to fit in. You'll read about people who could never hold down a traditional job because they pushed boundaries, refused to accept mediocrity, and demanded better.

You'll meet founders, creatives and leaders whose unconventional paths have reshaped industries. Some are household names; some are people making waves in their field and achieving incredible things. The common theme is how their grit and determination have helped them grow and contributed to their success.

This book is a celebration, a challenge, and a call to action. It's time to move beyond the label.

Together, we can remove the stigma and change the narrative.

Bringing These Stories Together

This book began as an initial spark of possibility that grew into the book you are holding now. The first conversations began, then Tasha joined the ADHD 360 family and from there, she took it from an idea to something real. After many conversations, interviews, and hours of listening to people willing to share their stories (the good, the bad and the unfiltered reality of living and working with ADHD), the book began to take shape into something truly special.

The people in this book were not chosen at random. Each one adds a different thread to the tapestry of stories we wanted to tell. Some are familiar faces whose names you may recognise or have seen on your screens. Others work quietly in the background, yet their impact is extraordinary, breaking Guinness World Records, embarking on life-changing adventures or reshaping the way businesses and public services operate.

Then there are those whose focus is deeply human, pouring their time and energy into helping others to grow and feel connected. They are the coaches, therapists and change-makers who stand alongside people in their most challenging moments, who champion the ADHD mission or simply make life better for the people they meet.

Every single one of them has a story worth telling and together they show just how many ways there are to leave your mark on the world. There is a common theme throughout; every one of these people share a refusal to let outdated ideas about ADHD limit what they can achieve.

Each story began with a conversation, often on WhatsApp and sometimes in person. We asked open and honest questions about life before diagnosis, the turning points that shaped their path and the highs and lows of running a business or working with an ADHD brain. Where we could, we also spoke to the people closest to them — partners, friends, and colleagues — to enrich the stories and give a full 360 view to their chapter.

With permission, each interview was recorded and transcribed using Otter.AI. This meant we could capture not just the words but also the rhythm, pauses and laughter that made each conversation unique. The transcripts became the foundation for the chapters you are about to read, ensuring the voice of each contributor came through exactly as they intended.

Once drafted, each narrative was refined with the contributor themselves, so it stayed true to the speaker's voice and experience. Every contributor has carefully reviewed and approved their chapter so what you read here is not just accurate but is genuinely their story in their own words.

This is not a clinical study. It is a carefully curated collection of stories told with honesty and care. The aim was never to create a polished highlight reel, it was to share the whole truth, with all its grit, vulnerability, humour, and brilliance.

By bringing these stories together, we hope they spark recognition, challenge stereotypes, and inspire you to see ADHD not as a limitation, but as a different way of moving through the world with its own strengths, struggles and extraordinary potential.

We hope that as you turn these pages, you find a story, a snippet or even just a single line that feels like it was written for you. Maybe you are exploring a diagnosis and feel apprehensive about what it might mean. Perhaps you have recently been diagnosed and have been left with no support, carrying the weight and grief that can sometimes come with that realisation. Perhaps you have known for a while, but find yourself at a crossroads, wanting to make a change but feeling anxious about taking that first step. Or maybe you are a parent of a neurodivergent child, and you worry about the world they are growing up in.

Wherever you are in your story, we want this book to be a companion, something that brings you comfort and helps you truly believe that ADHD is not the end. With the right understanding and support and with the right people around you, it can be the beginning of unlocking a life you might never have imagined possible.

So, let's begin. Let us introduce you to the people rewriting what it means to live beyond the label.

CHAPTER 1

The Founders & Visionaries*

*In this chapter, we introduce the people who saw a gap, a need, or a possibility and decided to act on it. They are the ones who built something from the ground up, often starting with little more than an idea and a determination to make it work.

Their journeys are filled with bold decisions, resilience and a refusal to be boxed in by other people's expectations.

Francesca James

Founder of Ideas Forums | Creator of Ideas Fest –
the 'Glastonbury for Business' | Building Communities &
Celebrating Entrepreneurs Shaping the Future

UNSTOPPABLE BY DESIGN

Francesca James, or Frankie, as she introduces herself, laughs when she explains what she does. "I run a business called Ideas Forums, which nobody's ever heard of," she says, "but what we actually do is build communities and put on events for incredible entrepreneurs all over the UK."

It's a modest description. In reality, Ideas Forums is home to the Great British Entrepreneur Awards, the UK Startup Awards, and Ideas Fest, affectionately known as the Glastonbury for Business. Frankie calls it their 'most quirky' creation, but it's a sell-out event that captures national attention – often selling out almost as quickly as the real Glastonbury.

Born and raised in Cardiff – where she still lives today, Frankie is a hugely successful entrepreneur, though you'd never guess it from the way she talks about her work. To understand how she got here, you have to go back to her school days, when she was known as the "could do better" kid.

She describes herself as an expert in winging it: masking in class, getting decent grades, but always with that same comment on her reports. Her attendance was poor, just 35% one year, something she managed to keep from her parents. Whilst she wasn't naturally academic, she enjoyed business studies and media. More than anything, she preferred working part-time, even when she was supposed to be at school.

By her teens, she was clocking serious hours at Halfords. Officially part-time, she took on so many shifts it was essentially full-time. "It probably explains why my attendance was so low," she jokes. Her pay packet gave her a huge buzz, and this piqued her interest far more than being at school.

That early taste of independence fuelled her drive but dulled her interest in academics. "I did ok in my exams, B's, C's and the odd A, mostly because my parents would catch me before I completely messed up and make me do hardcore revision," she says.

As the oldest child, Frankie was expected to be the first in her family to go to university, but she wasn't sure what she wanted. "I wasn't afraid to leave home, I actually thought I'd live on the other side of the world, but I was the only one of my siblings that actually ended up staying in Cardiff. Most of my friends went to uni and it would have made sense, but I just didn't know what I wanted to do, so I didn't."

Instead, she took a door-to-door sales job in the South Wales Valleys, working on 100% commission. She thrived. "The buzz of a sale was addictive, I was first in the office and last at the party," she says. For two years, she kept up the pace, but eventually realised the business was a pyramid scheme. She realised that although progressing into the roles above her and potentially getting the cars, holidays, and further promotions, it wasn't what she wanted and so she walked away.

With no plan for what to do next, she decided that now might be the time to go to university. It might be a way to create headspace and figure out her next move. She decided that because she enjoyed History and Politics, this is what she would study. Because she was in a relationship at the time, staying in Cardiff made sense.

What she quickly realised, however, was that most people on her course - straight out of school and a few years younger than her, except for a 70-year-old mature student - were well versed and already had a far deeper understanding of the subject. She learned to mirror those around her to mask her lack of knowledge. It was a challenge, but one she pulled off.

Through the course, she had a few wobbles, but her boyfriend at the time grounded her and encouraged her to persevere. She started working for her dad's company part-time and later launched her own business – a Content Agency - from the university library. This gave her the 'dopamine hit' her brain was missing from her degree and fuelled her determination to finish.

The agency grew. She had three staff, an office, and some high-profile clients, but with her dad's business as one of her biggest clients, scaling wasn't realistic. She went back to work with her dad and together in 2012, they launched the Great British Entrepreneur Awards.

A few years later, she raised the funds to buy the awards outright, running them independently. This marked the start of the ecosystem that would become Ideas Forums.

Where the awards cemented her credibility, Ideas Fest unlocked her creativity. Frankie first came up with the idea during the pandemic. It was bold, brave, and completely Frankie. When many businesses were focused on survival, Frankie wanted to create a space for entrepreneurs to reconnect, and she was determined it wouldn't look like the usual "conference hall with token bunting". Instead, she wanted something vibrant, fun, and immersive that felt like a proper festival.

The first festival in 2022 was a pilot. Rather than rushing straight into 2023, Frankie paused to assess the post-pandemic landscape and adapt to new timelines, guidance and understand what her audience wanted. Then in 2024, the second Ideas Fest was bigger, better, stronger and a sell-out.

Surprisingly, Frankie was only recently diagnosed with ADHD. She says the breadcrumbs were always there, but no one had joined the dots. Like many late-diagnosed women, she began to suspect something was different when ADHD became more visible on social media. Friends sent her memes they thought were 'so her' and after a year, she started to wonder if her misconception of ADHD as 'the naughty boy at school' was wrong.

At Ideas Fest 2024, she met keynote speaker Phil Anderton, CEO of ADHD360. With far more credibility than the social media content she'd seen, she talked to Phil about her experience and her suspicion, and he encouraged her to explore a diagnosis. Because they later formed a business partnership, Frankie put it at the top of her to-do list and got it done. Her diagnosis came earlier this year, just five days before she appeared on the Beyond the ADHD Label TV programme, giving a completely different perspective to her interview.

When it comes to ADHD, Frankie describes her hyperfocus as both a strength and a challenge. She works at lightning speed when something excites her but also uses it to avoid less appealing tasks, like tidying, organising, or planning travel. She's grateful that Dylan, her partner in both life and business, is the yang to her yin, balancing her out.

At work, Frankie is the ideas person. She brings energy, sparks interest with clients and then hands projects over to her team to deliver. They know she's not the detail person, but also that she has 'founder's disease', wanting to keep an eye on everything. They support her empathetically.

Like many with ADHD, Frankie finds it hard to say no. It's helped her pull off things others might think impossible and connect with incredible people, but it's also left her perpetually exhausted and living with little structure. Thankfully, her partner, friends, family, and team 'just get her'.

Her biggest strength is building connections. From her university content agency to the Great British Entrepreneur Awards, she's been able to spot talent before it becomes mainstream, connect people, and facilitate opportunities. She does this not as a strategy, but because she genuinely loves it.

For those starting out in entrepreneurship, especially fellow 'neurospicy' founders, Frankie's advice is simple: "Seek out the stories of people you admire. You'll see that even the most successful people are still figuring it out. They have vulnerabilities, struggles, messy lives, just like you and me."

If she could go back to her younger self, she'd repeat her dad's words: "You're as good as anybody, better than most." And she'd remind herself of her dad's words: "Nobody has it all figured out, but if they can do it, you can too." And she also says that she always tries to remember the well-known saying, "Everything will be okay in the end. If it's not okay, it's not the end."

Website:	ideasfest.uk
	greatbritishentrepreneurawards.com
	startupawards.uk
Instagram:	@frankie_j4y
LinkedIn:	@frangbea

John Reynolds

Entrepreneur | Investor | TV & Podcast Host & Creator | Relationship Director JAAQ | Host of Sky's Extraordinary Life Stories | Founder Titan Property Developments Ltd

UNSTOPPABLE BY DESIGN

When you first meet John, his warmth and charisma are infectious. He introduces himself simply: a serial entrepreneur, investor, and creator. Always learning. Naturally curious.

His story is one of graft, determination, and success, but the path has been anything but straightforward. He founded and scaled Titan Property Developments into a multi-million-pound business, partnering with billionaires and raising close to £50 million in equity.

He is well known for his warm and friendly interview style as the creator of Extraordinary Life Stories, which broadcasts on Bloomberg/SKY TV, where he has sat down with guests ranging from Stephen Fry to Damon Hill to Julia Bradbury. More recently, he co-created and co-hosts ADHD: Beyond the Label with Phil Anderton, CEO of ADHD360 — work he describes as the most fulfilling he has ever done.

John grew up in a loving but strict household. His father worked as Head of Car Safety at the Department of Transport, his mother was a dedicated housewife, and both grandfathers had been senior figures in the military, a brigadier in the Army and a wing commander in the RAF. Naturally, discipline, routine, and structure were central to his upbringing, with good manners and chivalry non-negotiable.

Active from a young age, John loved sport, riding his bike, and exploring further and further from home. At 13, he followed family tradition and was sent to boarding school. He found it restrictive and confining. While many of his peers thrived in the academic environment, John felt distracted, restless, and disengaged. Algebra and Bunsen burners felt meaningless. Passing exams to get a job held no attraction when he couldn't imagine what job he wanted. This left him in constant trouble: missed lessons, forgotten homework, endless detentions.

"I wasn't a bad kid, but I just didn't feel like I belonged anywhere in school. If something interested me, I excelled. But most of school didn't hold my interest."

Looking back now, as a late-diagnosed adult, John sees these as the early signs of ADHD.
Unlike many of his peers who went to university to pursue careers in law, medicine, or banking, John had no clear path. Instead, he sought his own journey, trying different jobs and travelling to India, China, and Egypt to seek culture and adventure.

He found his passion in sales. It suited his love of meeting people, building relationships, and being rewarded for effort. "People bought from me because they bought into me." This understanding gave him validation and momentum.

By his early twenties, John had left corporate sales in London, moving to Sandbanks in Poole to be near the sea - a lifelong love, testing himself with a commission-only sales role. He earned well, built up proper resilience and a strong local network - and met his future wife. Through those connections, he discovered property development and quickly realised he could thrive. He loved the creativity, the social aspect, and most of all, the relationship-building at its core.

Ambitious and restless, John spotted an opportunity in the 2013 amendment to Town and Country Planning legislation, which allowed office-to-residential conversions. He sourced opportunities off-market, recruited a best-in-class team, and raised close to £50 million from investors. In time, he was involved in over £260 million GDV of property development.

But the path wasn't easy. Deals were stolen by investors, trusted consultants passed opportunities through side doors, planning challenges stacked up, and legal due diligence often ground progress to a halt. John thrived on the chaos, taking on obstacles as professional challenges.

Then came the crises he couldn't control. The Grenfell tragedy created huge uncertainty around cladding, with the confusing and inconsistent introduction of the EWS1 form. Covid reshaped the housing market overnight, people suddenly wanted outdoor space, not town-centre flats. Confidence collapsed, interest rates rose, and buyers disappeared.

John realised he was ready to pivot. He wanted to move towards something more fulfilling.

He began investing in start-ups like Cudo and JAAQ, adding not just capital but connections, ideas, and leadership support. This tapped into his greatest passion: connecting people and creating opportunities. Surrounded by founders and entrepreneurs, he discovered a new energy and belonging, the camaraderie of risk-takers and creative thinkers.

In 2024, at Ideas Fest, John had a turning point. Before his own talk, he wandered into a packed marquee and heard Phil Anderton speaking about ADHD. The words resonated deeply. Later, John sought Phil out, and the conversation that followed sparked trust, understanding, and eventually, the idea for ADHD: Beyond the Label. Within weeks, filming began.

Guests including Christine McGuinness, Alex Partridge, Heston Blumenthal, and Frankie James joined them, sharing conversations that removed shame and built understanding. For John, it was transformational, not just as a platform, but as a mirror. He found himself saying, "I do that" and "I know what you mean." Curiosity became certainty, and soon he went through ADHD360 for an assessment.

The diagnosis came back positive. And for John, it was a moment of clarity.

"With everything I'd learnt, and the community I'd become part of, it felt like my tribe. If it had been negative, I think I'd have been left more confused than ever."

His diagnosis reframed his story. It explained the school struggles, the restlessness, the paperwork chaos, and also the boundless energy, creativity, empathy, and ability to connect quickly and deeply with others.

It also gave him permission to be kinder to himself. For years, his harshest critic had been his own inner voice. "I've always been cruel to myself at times," he admits. Now, he works at self-compassion, patience, and forgiveness.

As a father to two teenage daughters, he is mindful that ADHD is hereditary and recognises familiar patterns in them. He wants to model not only resilience but kindness.

John no longer defines success in one dimension. Titan Property gave him financial success and credibility, even proving experts wrong with record-breaking schemes. But personal success comes from storytelling, connection, and impact. Through Extraordinary Life Stories and ADHD: Beyond the Label, he wakes each day with a sense of purpose that no property deal could provide.

"The filming days with Phil are phenomenal. We both leave buzzing."

He believes his greatest achievement is still to come — "pulling people together on a mission-led basis."

John now embraces ADHD as both a superpower and a challenge. The relentless energy, hyperfocus, creativity, and relationship-building are strengths. The chaos, admin struggles, and tendency to start too many things remain challenges. But the difference is, he has reframed them. He leans into what helps him thrive, softens what hinders, and forgives himself more often.

His advice to entrepreneurs with ADHD is simple: "You are more capable than you think. Take small, consistent steps. Back yourself. Embrace failure as progress. ADHD gives you energy and hyperfocus, use them. You'll never regret backing yourself."

And to his teenage self? "Don't listen to people who call you a disappointment. Find what excites you and go after it relentlessly.

You don't need to fit the mould. Back yourself, seek experiences, and trust your gut."

Website:	extraordinarylifestories.com
Instagram:	@johnareynolds
LinkedIn:	@johnreynolds1

Jordan Wylie MBE

Award-winning adventurer | International bestselling author |
UK National Ambassador for Army Cadets

UNSTOPPABLE BY DESIGN

When people think of ADHD, the stereotype of naughty schoolboys who can't sit still is still very much the stereotype that springs to mind. And for Jordan Wylie, that's exactly how he describes his younger self.

A self-confessed cheeky, endlessly chatty, and restless 'handful' according to his teachers who described him as disruptive, always the joker and staring out of the window dreaming of doing anything but what he was supposed to.

Jordan introduces himself as "a former soldier but these days I'm an adventurer and author. Although, when people ask me what I do, if I'm honest I don't really know!" That short sentence captures the essence of who Jordan is. Someone who has had great success, achieved some incredible things and yet is still extraordinarily humble.

There is an obvious transition in his life from a structured military world to one that is now fuelled by risk, resilience, relentless energy, and a quiet determination to do good in the world, and to be a good role-model for people like him.

Whilst his initial description of his school days is one that most would describe as a typical ADHD kid, you can tell that for Jordan, this was just part of who he was, and he was just trying to get on and find where he fitted. He describes how he didn't really enjoy school "unless I was playing football, I'd be somewhere else in my head."

He left with very few qualifications and as such, his path was limited. The academic children went onto college or university, but for children like Jordan, if you didn't end up in prison, the options were likely apprenticeships or join the military. At 16, Jordan joined the army and for him, this shaped who he is now, and he is grateful for the life experiences and the personal development it afforded him. "The biggest thing I learned in the army was values. Understanding what they are and how to live by them."

He spent a decade in the army travelling the world, seeing some great places, some not-so-great places and had incredible times, but also horrific times. He made friends for life and developed a resilient determination in spite of the many challenges and difficult times that would come. After 10 years, he decided to leave and from there had to learn how to live in a completely different environment.

Life outside the forces felt disorientating. "When you're in the army, you don't realise how important the structure is. Even polishing your boots or pressing your kit. Once it's gone, you miss it." Without that structure and routine, Jordan struggled with his identity and purpose. He had to re-learn who he was and what would come next and as time passed, he realised he could build a life around the things he loved - adventure and the outdoors - and build a life creating a positive impact on the world. "I'll never be rich in money, but I am rich in experiences and purpose. I live a happy, healthy-enough life."

Looking back, there were signs of what he now understands as ADHD. At the time it just felt like 'being Jordan'. He was the cheeky one, the joker, the football captain. Sport carried him through, both at school and later in the army. "If you were good at sport, you were given a bit of leeway," he explains. He laughs as he recalls his sergeant major's words when he was promoted to lance corporal after just two and a half years: "I wish I was good at football. I had to work a lot harder for my first stripe than you did." This stuck with him, and he has always worked hard to ensure that any successes he has achieved, he has worked hard for them.

Jordan notes how he has always had a brain that liked to push boundaries not because he was a troublemaker but because it was who he was – part of his DNA. "I wasn't consciously testing how much I could get away with. It's just how I was wired. I've always thought differently, I've never been afraid to go off the beaten track."

Even completing his many adventures, Jordan was never interested in doing it for the recognition or accolades but instead wanted to do something new, challenging, that had never been done before.

"Lots of athletes and adventurers want to break records or push boundaries. I'm more interested in doing something no one has done before, or going somewhere no one has been. That's always been my mentality."

At age 41, Jordan finally got his formal diagnosis of ADHD. "It was quite a relief, actually. It answered a lot of questions about why I am the way I am, why I've made certain decisions, why I struggle in certain environments and excel in others. I'm very impulsive, that's been both a strength and a weakness.

He describes how his ADHD has been both gift and challenge. "In my adventures, ADHD has been a gift. I thrive in chaos and uncertainty, I'm not afraid to take risks and I can hyperfocus when I'm passionate about something. But it's also caused challenges in relationships, in being present, in staying organised. I've lost opportunities and relationships because of it. But now I understand it better, I can work with it rather than against it."

He knows that his 'way' has been challenging for those around him and whilst they love him unconditionally, it may have helped if he'd had an earlier diagnosis. "I'm sure my family would have wanted that. I've given some people a tough ride. I've done things and said things I regret. Maybe life would have been different. But I wouldn't change anything now, even if others might."

When thinking about parts of his ADHD that he would maybe like to have a bit more control over, he pauses and shares that it would be to have the ability to switch off. "I never stop. Even when I'm at home, I'm on the laptop, chasing sponsors, doing interviews. And I love it, that's the problem. But it means I'm never fully present with my loved ones. If I could change one thing, it would be to give them all my attention. That would make them happier, and in turn, me too."

His advice to others newly diagnosed with ADHD is simple but powerful: "Embrace the chaos, use it to your advantage. Harness those positive traits into one big push and back yourself. Believe in yourself before expecting others to believe in you."

He also adds a cautionary note though. "The danger with ADHD is spreading your energy too thin, saying yes to too much, trying to please everyone. That dilutes what you can achieve. You have to prioritise what really matters and channel your energy into that.

Protect your energy and don't give it away to people who don't deserve it."

When thinking back to his own childhood, particularly his teenage years, if he could go back and give himself some advice, his answer is clear and filled with perspective:

"Buckle in because it's going to be an epic adventure. Life is a privilege. If you're living and breathing, you're already in a privileged position. So many people would give anything for one more day, one more meal, one more hug. You don't have to have it all figured out. I'm 42 and I don't know what the next year holds. I still don't know what I want to be when I grow up!"

As an adventurer, he's often asked if it's about the journey or the destination. His response is delivered with absolute certainty. "Neither. It's about the people. Surround yourself with good, positive people. That's what really matters. My favourite places and my adventures aren't about the location; they're about the people I was with."

Whilst being late diagnosed has brought validation and a renewed sense of self, Jordan is also able to see the positives that have come out of the challenges he's experienced. The challenges have taken on a different meaning as time has passed.

"When you're young, you tend to see stumbling blocks. With perspective, you see opportunities hidden inside them. Every obstacle can be a stepping stone."

That's the message that fuels Jordan's internal narrative now. A restless, risk-taking spirit can become a gift once you learn to work with it. His story is proof that ADHD doesn't have to be a barrier – it can be the very thing that fuels the adventure.

Website: jordanwylie.org
Instagram: @mrjordanwylie
LinkedIn: @jordanwylie

Nick Hollis

Motivational Speaker | Seven Summiteer | ICF certified Life Coach |
721 Challenge for World Land Trust

UNSTOPPABLE BY DESIGN

At first glance, Nick Hollis is calm, steady, and humble. Look closer, and you find a man fuelled by ambition and a relentless drive to achieve the extraordinary. He chuckles when asked to sum up what he does, finding it hard to distil into a single sentence: "I'm an adventurer, professional speaker, mountain guide, and founder of a training and expedition company."

He's also in the final stages of a world record attempt, the 721 Challenge, which involves climbing the Seven Summits, skiing to the North and South Poles and rowing the Atlantic Ocean. Nine are complete. One remains: the elusive, unrelenting, and unforgiving North Pole. Nick explains. "Nine out of ten are done. One remains. It's my nemesis, my ball and chain."

Alongside expeditions, he now focuses on building a high-performing team development programme, translating lessons from extreme environments back into the business world. Coaching and leadership are as much part of his work as the mountains.

As a child, Nick describes how he was 'good on paper' but deep down, he had deep-rooted internal anxiety, feeling like a square peg in a round hole. "If it was a subject I enjoyed, I'd come home with glowing reports, top of the class. If it wasn't, I was a liability. My school reports almost looked like they were describing two different people."

He describes how he never really slept as a child and that from around 12, he would often wander out into the countryside late at night to help calm his brain. "I couldn't switch off. I'd go walking at ten o'clock and come home at two in the morning. That was the only way my mind calmed itself enough to sleep."

The middle child, with one older and one much younger brother, he describes growing up as being focused on security and stability and less on emotional awareness. "My parents came from a different era. They weren't unkind, but they didn't really see or understand the difference. They gave me space, though, and in hindsight that was important."

Nick's ADHD realisation came many years later, in 2019 when he was on an expedition climbing Mount Vinson in Antarctica. On top of the mountain, another climber, also a successful entrepreneur, confided in Nick that he had ADHD, then looked at Nick and said, "And of course, so have you".

Nick recalls getting home from that trip, jumping straight onto Dr Google where every ADHD questionnaire and test that he could find, he completed. "They all came back the same. That comment had stuck with me."

Nick then began the painfully slow process of being referred for assessment through the NHS Right to Choose pathway. Eventually, he reached the top of the list and was assessed and had his diagnosis confirmed, by ADHD360, in 2022. He recalls "When they told me, I said to them I'd have been more surprised if they'd told me I didn't have ADHD. It just made so much sense of my life."

Nick shares how helpful medication has been for him in managing his ADHD, particularly whilst undertaking expeditions. When he completed the South Pole element of his 721 Challenge, he recorded a video for ADHD360 thanking them for the support they'd given him and how much getting this diagnosis and subsequent support and treatment had changed his life. "That was really the start of my ADHD360 partnership. Phil saw the video and reached out. We've been working together ever since."

Prior to becoming the Adventurer that Nick is today, he had built a very successful corporate career with Hewlett Packard and reflects that "I rose to the top 1% of performers in the company, but the personal cost was immense. I was working 15-hour days, weekends and even Christmas Day. I survived by being the best. That bought me leniency and managers left me alone because they knew I would deliver. But the personal cost was burnout, and it was unsustainable."

After some time, he made the difficult decision to walk away. There was no redundancy, no golden handshake, just a brave decision that the personal cost was too high. "It was probably the most courageous thing I've ever done. That choice changed everything".

Nick then focused on rebuilding his health, retraining in outdoor pursuits and eventually set up Fitways Adventures to enable him to safely support people to explore their own outdoor interests. That company evolved into the 721 Challenge that remains his nemesis but also fuelled his decision to set up the 721 Leadership Academy.

As someone who had experienced a successful corporate career but at personal cost, the 721 Leadership Academy was Nick's way of bringing the mountains into the boardroom. He contributes its success to the many lessons that he's learned in his outdoor adventures, at altitude. The need for resilience, adaptability, teamwork under pressure are all key skills needed to succeed both in the high-stakes expeditions, but also in the boardroom. These fundamentals became the foundation of Nick's leadership programme designed for executives and teams.

"I'm not just providing a motivational speech, I'm showing leaders what happens when stress hits, when conditions change without warning and you have to rely on the person next to you. The outdoors gives you those lessons fast and without ego."

Nick's ability to blend his expedition experiences with his natural coaching style into a simulation-type session exploring the physical and mental challenges you might face is unparalleled in the leadership development space. "It's about building leaders who are prepared, not just on paper but in reality. Leaders who can adapt, problem-solve, and support others in uncertainty."

The Academy shows how much Nick has developed through his own ADHD journey, too. He has had to harness the strengths and overcome the challenges that being neurodivergent presents. He's harnessed the intensity, channelled his hyperfocus and reframed the struggles he's experienced into the strength of who he is today. "What I've learned in the wild is what I wish I'd been taught at school. Different doesn't mean broken. Different can mean powerful."

Whilst Nick has taken his diagnosis and what that means in his stride, he describes it as both a gift and a burden. Thinking about the strengths it provides him, he describes a relentless energy and drive, the ability to form a vision and take that first step. Hyperfocus switches on in extreme situations whether that's mountain rescues or corporate crises and overall, the ability to remain calm under pressure. The flip side of that though is that he finds it impossible to switch off without feeling guilty. He feels inconsistent sharing, "some days I'm brilliant, others I can't get going," and relies a lot on his stress hormones and adrenaline to keep him going which long-term can be problematic. His sleep is disrupted, and he struggles with impulsive eating. He is also his own harshest critic and has a complete inability to celebrate his achievements. He describes how "Every day feels like a blank sheet of paper. Whatever I did yesterday doesn't matter. That can drive achievement, but it's exhausting. The diagnosis gave me compassion. It let me forgive myself. That's been huge."

Whilst he acknowledges and accepts his ADHD is part of who he is, he reflects that "I would love to be able to flick the hyperfocus switch on and off myself instead of it being dictated by circumstance."

Without question, Nick has lived a life of extremes, and his expeditions truly reflect both sides of ADHD – the good and the more challenging. He recalls that whilst summiting Everest in 2019, he realised he'd damaged his eyes. "I was blind on the summit of Everest. Most people would have panicked but my ADHD superpower kicked in. I was calm, coherent, able to plan my way down with my guide. That saved me."

And yet, that same brain that thrives in crises and chaos, forbids him to experience calm and balance. His evenings are often spent feeling exhausted as his medication wears off and his social time is sacrificed with work or recovery. "I think my friends probably wish I was more available and present. But when they do see me, it's usually healthy time and we go walking or training, not out drinking. I suppose I'm good for their wellbeing too!"

When asked what advice Nick would give to others starting their own ADHD journey – whether in business, or as a newly diagnosed person looking to take more control over their life, he shares that you should "take time to really connect with who you are. Your ADHD superpower will only work if driven by authenticity".

He suggests that having a vision or a compass that harnesses your energy, doing one thing at a time (keeping it simple!), protecting your energy and setting boundaries are critical. Most of all though, he explains the importance of celebrating success. "Even though I struggle with it, it's vital."

Thinking back to himself as a teenager, Nick says he would keep it simple: "Enjoy it. Give yourself permission to enjoy the journey."

Website: nickhollis.com
Instagram: @nickhollis721
LinkedIn: @nickhollis721

Emma Sayle

CEO KK Group | Killing Kittens | Founder |
The Sisterhood | Public Speaker

Emma laughs as she begins her story, explaining to me that she's picking up dog poo at the very moment the conversation begins. The timing, she says, is always the same. As soon as she starts a meeting, the dog decides to do its business. It's a fitting start really: grounded, unfiltered, and entirely her.

Today, she is best known as the founder of the KK Group, a collection of businesses designed to empower people sexually. What started as a bold move to challenge the male dominance of the adult industry has grown into a movement: parties, cruises, retreats, and the Sisterhood which is a community that encourages women into extreme sports and wild adventures. For nearly two decades, she has been dismantling shame and rewriting the rules of sexual empowerment.

But to understand who Emma is today, it's important to understand her story of getting here.

As a child, Emma moved every two years with her father's army and Foreign Office roles, living in places like Egypt, Kuwait, and Berlin. At eight, her parents decided boarding school would bring stability, and she remained there until 18. She excelled academically, achieving straight A's, captaining sports teams and eventually becoming head of house.

Yet home life was tense. Her father, a Cambridge scholar, was old-school, controlling, and quick-tempered. Emma found him emotionally abusive and often clashed with him, shielding her younger siblings and refusing to accept his injustice. She describes how her mother, vibrant and social, was boxed in for decades.

Emma was always fiery, questioning rules and pushing back against authority. At school, she even organised strikes when weekly weigh-ins were introduced, furious at the public humiliation. Determined and tomboyish, she refused to accept that girls were less than boys. If they climbed trees, so would she. As a teenager, she channelled her rage at inequality, a force that later fuelled her mission to level the playing field in the most taboo of arenas: sex.

Her husband reflects that this determination has always defined her: "She's incredibly driven. If it's a noble cause or something that sparks her, she'll come out biting. That drive is her biggest trait, and it's why she never stands still."

Outwardly, Emma was unstoppable. She could read a text once and recall it word for word, and school was never difficult. Yet behind her high achievement lay a need to fit in and excel at everything. She carried the weight of wanting to make her dad proud, recalling how "an A was never good enough; it had to be an A+." By her mid-teens, this perfectionism became an eating disorder that lasted a decade, her way of coping with relentless pressure.

At 18, she went to university to study Sports Science, where she discovered her true passion: the social world. She was the Lacrosse club captain, President of the Cocktail Society, and a natural ringleader. Frustrated by the Athletic Union's structure, she set about changing it, saying, "if it wasn't right, I would do it differently." That mentality, to challenge and reshape, has defined her path to who she is today.

After graduating, Emma briefly entered the world of advertising and PR but quickly realised she was unemployable. She had some short-term jobs selling ad space and working in financial PR, but later moved into personal training and then, impulsively, a move abroad at age 22.

Emma's move to Curaçao marked a turning point. Choosing to leave an abusive relationship, she built a new start as head trainer at a gym. Within a year she was back in the UK, freelancing in entertainment PR, where she found herself on the peripheries of the adult entertainment industry.

Just as she had at university, Emma refused to accept inequality in the professional world. She saw women's brands run entirely by men; sex parties designed for male gratification and porn catering only to male desire. Determined to change it, she set out to turn the industry on its head and bring true equality.

A few years later, at a wedding abroad, a friend teased that the group were all 'sitting around killing kittens', a cheeky euphemism for masturbation. The line stuck, and it became the spark for Emma's revolutionary brand, Killing Kittens. Emma had found her calling creating a world where women were in control and free from shame or judgment. Her first party drew just 40 people, but within weeks, the media attention exploded. In the early 2000s, as society tentatively began to acknowledge female sexual agency, Emma pushed it further than anyone had dared.

What began as quiet whispers soon grew into a global movement. Killing Kittens now counts over 250,000 members worldwide, and Emma regularly hears from women who left abusive relationships, rediscovered lost parts or parts they didn't even know existed after attending KK events. Her vision gave them the confidence to reclaim their power.

Emma shares how much of her growth and success would not have been possible without her ADHD brain. She describes how she sees the full 'chessboard of possibility'. Whilst others are obsessing over details, she was spotting societal trends years in advance; she can adapt and pivot quickly and can visualise the bigger picture. She admits, however, 'I'm not a detail person, I'm impatient and want to get on with it," and notes that having a business partner who thrives on detail has been critical to allow her to balance her visionary energy and focus on strategy and creativity. Her husband recognises this too: "She sees a problem, and she'll go and fix it, diving deep until she finds the answer. She's never been one to just accept what others tell her; she needs to test it, prove it, and push until she's satisfied. That's why she's able to challenge entire industries."

Emma didn't get her ADHD diagnosis until her early 30s, and this was prompted by a conversation with a journalist. In an interview, they hinted at it, but Emma brushed it off, feeling it was an explanation rather than a label. It wasn't until two decades later, with the overwhelm of having three young children and the hormonal chaos that comes with perimenopause, that Emma revisited it. Her assessment was clear. She began taking medication and within weeks, she describes how she felt the shift as transformative. "Before, my brain was like dodgems. Now it's Clapham Junction. The trains are still moving fast, but they're on tracks. I can jump between them without chaos."

She explains that the biggest impact, though, has been her relationship with her children. Previously, the meltdowns they experienced would have pushed her to the edge, but now she can respond with calmness and compassion and the ability to walk away briefly when needed, rather than meeting it with equal chaos. "That's been huge for me".

Her husband sees that same strength at home: "She's the glue that holds everything together. The kids' clubs, the holidays, the house, it all runs because of her hyperfocus. She does it almost without thinking — it's her superpower."

Emma is clear on how her ADHD fuels her drive, her creativity, and her refusal to accept 'that's just the way it is'. It's her engine. She shares how she is proud that she can remain calm in chaos and visualise the bigger picture. She shares how others are swept up with her contagious energy. However, she also shares the reality of ADHD, the difficulties that come with the positives. She struggles with being overwhelmed, and impatient and taking things too personally but learning how to set boundaries and, professionally, to lean on her team. "The best thing I ever did was surround myself with people better than me at the things I'm not good at." She says that if she could go back to herself as a teenager, she would tell herself without question, "You are enough. You don't have anything to prove."

He adds that part of what makes their relationship work is balance: "I'm naturally more relaxed, where Emma wants things done now. That intensity can be challenging, but it's also what pushes us forward. Her energy doesn't allow life to ever be dull."
From a party of 40 people to a business celebrating its 20th anniversary, she has built something remarkable. She was the first to crowdfund in the adult sector, the first to launch a cruise

dedicated to women's empowerment and the first to transform the taboo into tech.

Her husband sums it up simply: "She doesn't give herself enough credit for what she's built. This isn't just a business; it's a community and a movement that has changed lives. People are better for knowing her."

What began as rage against unfairness and inequality has become a global movement of confidence, liberation, and community. Her ADHD has been both a challenge and a superpower, but she wouldn't change it.

"People say ADHD is an excuse," she reflects. "It's not an excuse. It's part of who I am. And it's given me the drive to create a world that didn't exist but desperately needed to."

Her husband's final word echoes this: "If she ever doubts herself, I tell her, take a breath, look around and see what you've built. It's phenomenal."

Website:	wearekk.com
Instagram:	@emsayle333
LinkedIn:	@emsayle

Ash Jones

Founder at Great Influence | Personal Brand Advisor

When you first meet Ash, he doesn't come across as chaotic at all. He's calm, measured, softly spoken. But the more you listen, the more you realise just how fast his brain works. If you asked his team, they'd probably describe him as calm, steady, and focused. Dig a little deeper, though, and you'll spot the signs of what he calls a 'chaos brain', a mind that rarely sits still. What's remarkable is not just what he's built, but how he's done it. He doesn't frame his ADHD as a barrier. It's clear from talking to him that it's quietly shaped the way he thinks, works, and leads, even before he had a name for it.

Ash is the founder of Great Influence, a personal branding agency working with some of the most recognisable names in business. Before that, he helped build the personal brand of Steven Bartlett, now a household name thanks to Diary of a CEO, Dragons' Den and more. He was one of the founding team at Social Chain, working behind the scenes before personal branding was even considered a 'thing'. Today, his agency represents clients like Gary Neville and leaders from companies like Booking.com, Diageo, Gousto, and Huel.

His story is seriously impressive, but his early years will feel familiar to a lot of neurodivergent (late-diagnosed) adults. "I got kicked out of my first primary school. I wasn't violent, but I threw a chair and a table at someone. I liked being on my own, in my bedroom. Not naughty, just rebellious."

Ash openly admits school didn't work for him. He left with one GCSE having skipped an exam to see Metallica, and then bounced between jobs, college courses, and restlessness. From 16 to 25, he couldn't hold down a job for more than a month. He had no qualifications and no clear direction. But something shifted at 24. He made the decision to go to university, and at a rap event with a friend, met someone who would change the course of his life: Steven Bartlett.

"I messaged him saying I'd heard networking was important, so this was me networking. I offered to help him for free while I was at uni."

That bold message led to a position on Steven's team, and eventually to Ash finding himself building Steve's personal brand, a role that didn't yet exist in the industry. At the time, building Steve's brand was just the most effective way to get his business out there, but it ended up becoming the start of something much bigger. He explains that he didn't set out to invent a new job title, but that's kind of what happened. He moved from marketing into what he now calls 'personal branding' and ended up building an entire business around it. And yet, it would be years before Ash realised that his success was, in part, because his brain was wired differently.

"I didn't even know what ADHD was." Ash was diagnosed with ADHD just a few years ago and only because he had hired Ellie Middleton, a neurodivergent activist and speaker, who was beginning to explore her own neurodivergent identity.

"I came at it from the perspective of being an employer. Ellie was going through something I didn't understand. So, I started learning about ADHD for her and ended up discovering it applied to me too." Like many late-diagnosed adults, Ash fell down a rabbit hole of research. But unlike others, the process didn't lead to grief or shock.

It simply made sense. "I'm into optimisation. I wear a Whoop band. I like tweaking my routines. ADHD became another piece of information I could use to improve how I operate. There was no trauma, just, 'Okay, cool. This explains a lot'."

That pragmatic attitude shows up throughout Ash's story. While the ADHD label helped give language to his experience, he didn't rewrite his past or dramatically overhaul his life. Instead, he made small, meaningful shifts, especially in how he works and manages his time. "Before I met Steve, I had the worst work ethic of anyone I knew. I had all this energy but nowhere to put it. Now, I've got direction and that same chaotic brain is my biggest strength."

Today, Ash's energy is channelled into high-level thinking, creative strategy, and supporting his team. His mind is still fast, still full, but now it's focused. "There was a time I managed ten clients alone. Now we've got a team of seven doing the same. But even with support, I tend to fill the space with more stuff. That's just how I'm wired."

That wiring is something his team knows well. Claudia, who has worked alongside him for five years and is now Strategy Director at Great Influence, describes him as one of the most generous, smart, and relentlessly forward-thinking people she's ever met. "His ability to predict what's going to happen next, culturally or in business, is second to none. He'll say something months in advance and then it happens. It's like he can see patterns no one else sees, and explain them so clearly that you immediately buy in."
Claudia recalls watching him navigate his ADHD diagnosis. "At first, he almost had to rewrite his history with this new lens, and that was difficult. But he decided early on, ADHD wasn't going to be an

excuse not to do things. If anything, it would be the reason he did them. He's used it as an advantage." She also points out his hyperfocus: "Great Influence has been his hyperfocus for years. It's why the agency is what it is today. He just thinks about it constantly and that's been invaluable for all of us."

But like Ash himself admits, it's not without challenge. "He's constantly pushing forward," Claudia says. "That drive is inspiring, but it can be relentless. Sometimes it's random impulsive things, two old TVs showing up in the office or booking a last-minute trip at 7am. But that's also the fun of working with him. He makes even the hardest moments enjoyable because there's always laughter alongside the pressure."

When asked what she admires most, Claudia highlights his ability to create genuine relationships. "Everyone loves being around Ash. From high-level CEOs to people he's just met, he treats everyone the same. He doesn't even realise how meaningful that is."

For Ash, what matters most is clarity, of thought, of communication, of focus. "If you're unclear, he'll press until you find the exact meaning," Claudia laughs. "At first, that was tough, but now it's a gift. It's made me a clearer thinker, and it's made our whole team stronger."

When asked if he feels understood, Ash credits the circles he moves in. Steven Bartlett. Ellie. His team. All of them, in some way, hold neurodivergent traits. That shared understanding has helped him feel less different and more grounded. "I feel quite normal because I'm around other crazy people too."

He says this with a smile, but the point runs deep. ADHD can feel isolating when you're surrounded by people who don't 'get it'. Listening to both Ash and Claudia, it's obvious how important it's been for him to be around other neurodivergent people. It's not just acceptance; it's a shared way of thinking that makes you feel like you actually fit somewhere.

Still, Ash admits he struggles with idea overload, starting new projects and then losing steam quickly. "I'll have an idea, then another, and another. It's hard to stick with just one. I get hyped at the beginning, then the momentum drops. That's a challenge."

But he's learning to manage it with support, structure, and self-awareness. His team knows how he works. His family steps in when life gets too busy. Claudia reflects on his journey with pride: "To see him go through a diagnosis, reframe his whole story, and come out even stronger is incredible. He's not defined by ADHD, but he's not ignoring it either. He's used it to level up."

And when asked what others might change about his ADHD? Ash answers simply: "Nothing. Maybe just, 'do a bit less'. But people accept me as I am. I'm really lucky in that."

When asked what advice he'd give to others just beginning their ADHD journey, Ash is clear: "Let it be a cog in the machine, not a spanner in the works." He doesn't romanticise ADHD, nor does he position it as a curse. It just is. He shares that if you can work with it, not against it, it can become a powerful part of who you are.

If there's one message Ash would give his younger self? "Chill out. It's going to take a little longer than you think. But you'll get there."

It's not about speed. It's about finding the right moment, the right focus, the right people to back you, and having the self-belief to follow through. Ash didn't take the traditional path, but his story proves that sometimes, that's exactly what leads you to the work you were meant to do.

Website: greatinfluence.com
Instagram: @ashleybjones
LinkedIn: @ash-jones-85363975

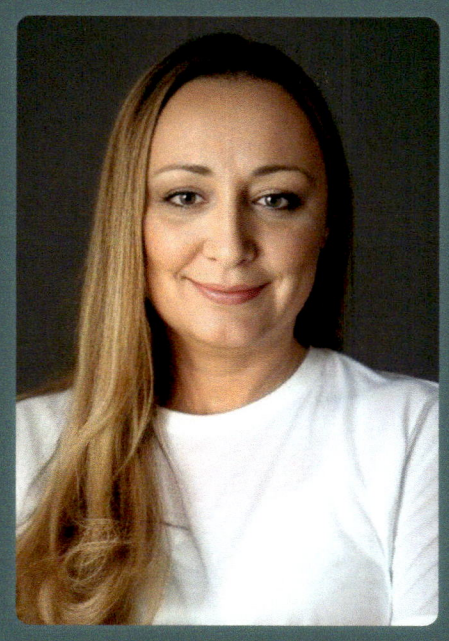

Katrina Hutchinson-O'Neill

CEO & Founder at Join Talent | Founder of #SheSaysMore

"First female-founded company to hit number one on the Times Growth List."

That sounds like a headline, but for Katrina Hutchinson-O'Neill, Katrina, it's just one part of her story. Behind the record-breaking £25 million turnover, the FT ranking and a team stretching across 26 countries, Katrina's restless brain never switches off.

When you speak to Katrina, she'll tell you straight, it wasn't a clever strategy or a perfectly crafted business plan that made her different; it was ADHD.

The same brain that leaves her frozen, staring at a to-do list, is the one that pushed her to build a company at a pace no one could have predicted.

Katrina's story has layers. To really understand her drive, you have to start with where she grew up.

Growing up in Northern Ireland during the Troubles was chaotic and unsettled. Katrina went to seven schools in 14 years, always the new kid, never feeling rooted anywhere. She remembers one headmaster who spotted something in her: potential. He gave her tougher textbooks, arranged early assessments, and pushed her further. She flew through it all and also got put up a year. "It was the happiest I'd ever felt in a classroom."

But that didn't last. A move to yet another school put her back with younger kids, starting from scratch. A headmaster who didn't think it was right she should be on track for university at 16. The boredom hit, frustration built and that spark disappeared. Restlessness turned into defiance. "What's the point?" became her mantra. Homework stopped, rules were ignored and the frustration she felt inside grew.

That same pattern played out later at university. Katrina had her sights set on Durham, but her parents didn't understand. They thought it was a polytechnic and insisted she go to Queen's University Belfast – a great uni but one that didn't offer her anything like the course she wanted to study. She lasted a year doing a subject she was not engaged on. "It was inevitable, really. Unless I found myself doing something I was absolutely passionate about, I was never going to stick it out."

So, she travelled, lived, casually worked across several countries, and then stumbled back home and immediately fell into the corporate world. At first, she excelled. Her ADHD traits, relentless energy, quick thinking, and a refusal to play by the 'this is how we do things' mantra helped her climb the ladder quickly.

But tension was never far away. One piece of feedback stuck: her "strengths are too strong."

Katrina laughs at the absurdity of it now. What they really meant was her ability to 'get shit done' didn't fit neatly into a world run by politics and hierarchy. She pushed people's buttons, she showed people up – neither intentionally, but in her constant ability to progress and deliver plus her early in career lack of finesse in understanding that not everyone was wired the way she was. She refused to play the game.

Six years ago, she walked away from corporate life. "It was crazy, but it also made perfect sense."

Her first company, Join Talent, exploded from £0 to £21 million turnover in three years. No investors, no debt, just Katrina and a growing handful of people who believed in her. From there came ThinkSpike, an e-learning platform for in-house recruiters, and now a third business is building in the background.

Work is only one part of her life though. Katrina is married with three kids, a cat, and three dogs and shares, "None of this would have been possible without my husband. He quit teaching when the business really took off to help me – took charge of the house, the kids and the dogs and became my scaffolding. He even manages the reporting and scheduling for the business itself." He's the steady structure behind her whirlwind energy.

Sharing more about being diagnosed with ADHD, Katrina recalls that when her youngest daughter turned four, ADHD really came into sharp focus. "She's me, just without the masking. She's unapologetic, restless, and full of quirks." Katrina wanted to help her but knew she would first have to understand herself.

Her first ADHD assessment was ridiculous: fifteen minutes, yes or no questions and a report emailed over. Yes, you have ADHD, but no support, no conversation. The second, with another organisation, several years later was the opposite. Hours of exhausting Zoom calls and endless hoops to jump through but still a positive diagnosis but no support and repeated no-shows by the provider for the treatment consultations.

In typical Katrina fashion, she found her own solution. On a trip to Mexico, frustrated and determined, she saw a doctor there. After hearing her story and reading through her diagnosis, he prescribed her ADHD medication. "It wasn't exactly the expected route, but it changed my life."

Katrina doesn't sugar-coat ADHD. She explains it's her superpower and her curse. The traits that let her leave competitors like rabbits in headlights can also leave her paralysed by the simplest of tasks.

She's smashed industry records and channelled hyperfocus into phenomenal results but equally, she can lose days researching pointless rubbish in a hyperfocus rabbit-hole. The medication, a short-acting version that she can take as and when needed, has been a saving grace in this respect.

There is one thing she struggles with because of her ADHD, above all else: misophonia (Defined as a "pathological disgust or anger triggered by a certain sound," Collins English Dictionary Online). Eating noises and repetitive visuals are constant triggers. "It's awful. If I could laser it out of my brain, I would. It serves absolutely no purpose."

Despite it all, ADHD is what makes Katrina unstoppable. Her proudest moment isn't the revenue or the FT ranking but getting the Times Growth List number one spot. "I didn't even know we were the first female-founded company to do it. I found out six months later, by accident. But that's the one I've actually stopped to reflect on."

Recognition matters. For her children, for other women, and for anyone who's ever been told their strengths are 'too strong.'

Asked what advice she'd give other ADHD entrepreneurs, she says: "Figure out what derails you. For some, it's spreadsheets. For me, it's endless to-do lists. Don't let those things sap your energy. Build safety nets. Find scaffolding. Protect your focus for the things that matter."

Katrina remembers being 14 and excelling in biology because she found it so interesting. She was getting A grades in that and some other subjects she loved, but in subjects like maths, chemistry, and physics, she scraped by with Bs or Cs. She remembers the headmaster pulling her up on the fact that she wasn't doing well in some subjects and dismissing her success in biology with a cruel, hurtful remark: "You're only doing well in biology because you fancy your teacher because he's a young and attractive guy". Katrina shares, "I'd never even thought about that. It was awful, untrue and I felt so much shame."

Rather than recognising what unlocked her learning, he reduced her achievement to a joke, and it knocked her confidence in a subject she loved. Katrina recognises that, particularly for a neurodivergent teenager, that could have been so damaging.

Looking back, Katrina knows that if someone had given her a vision for the future and shown her how to harness her brain, she could have achieved anything. That moment of shame now fuels her determination to ensure her children get the scaffolding and support she never had.

Katrina is living proof that when you believe anything is possible, you can move mountains. The difference for her children is that they can too, and they'll never have to do it alone.

Website: jointalent.net
LinkedIn: @recruit2
Instagram: @jointalent

Paul Thandi CBE DL

Private Equity Investor & Board Member | Former CEO and
Chairman at NEC Group | Non-Executive Director |
Chair of multiple businesses

"All my life I've had this voice in my head telling me I could do better," Paul shares. "At 59, to be told that was ADHD, that I wasn't on my own, that others were the same, it was a big shift."

Paul Thandi isn't your average late-diagnosed entrepreneur. He's spent decades at the sharp end of business, a Private Equity Investor and Board Member, CEO of the NEC Group, and now a Non-Executive Director and Chair across multiple industries from hospitality to healthcare to sustainable energy.

Along the way, he's been awarded a CBE and appointed Deputy Lieutenant, a formal recognition of a career built on relentless determination, backing himself and pushing boundaries.

For Paul, though, those titles aren't what define him. The ADHD diagnosis came after decades of building and selling businesses, leading teams, and reinventing himself more than once, or, as he puts it with a grin, "running them like they're still a corner shop, hustling". By any measure, he's been successful. But what's the thing he counts as real success? That his grown-up kids still want to sit around a table with him, still ring him for advice and still laugh with him.

For years, Paul's life ran on structure. His coping strategy was simple: keep a full diary and always have a plan for the weekend. "If there wasn't a plan, I couldn't cope," he explains. "It could change, that wasn't the issue, but I had to know what I was doing." Training in the morning gave him balance but the rhythm of being busy kept him steady.

Then there was this internal voice, his inner narrative. Not textbook imposter syndrome that people talk about, but something deeper. His was a relentless inner critic telling him he could have done better.

It was only after being diagnosed with ADHD that he realised how many other people live with the same thing. Entrepreneurs, he describes in particular, "Brilliant at work, devoted to their families, but bloody hard to live with!" he says. "They are restless, intense, always driving forward. That's the reality."

Two weeks after his diagnosis, Paul tried ADHD medication for the first time. "For the first time in 59 years, I couldn't hear anything in my head. I just sat on the sofa. Not because I'd given up, not because I was exhausted, but because I could. I was comfortable. That was emotional."

He came off the initial medication quickly finding the side effects, particularly the insomnia, too much. But having had that moment of silence in his head, that internal chatter gone, was revelatory for him. He switched to a shorter-acting stimulant that felt less harsh on his system and a better fit for his needs. "I don't need it to last all day. I just need enough to get me through the parts that matter."

In childhood, Paul grew up in London. He was the son of Indian parents who arrived in the UK the 1960s. His father was an accountant for the government, and his mother was a hospital theatre nurse. Both had a fierce work ethic, and he remembers his childhood as free, happy, and full of laughter.

"We didn't have much, but we had a lot of freedom. Summers were spent out all day, playing football, with mates, just constant noise, and energy."

Academically, Paul was bright and capable but often lacked interest or engagement. He failed most of his O-levels the first time round, not through lack of ability but because the work simply didn't interest him. When he went back, he passed them all with ease and even became head boy; proof that when something captured his attention, he could excel. That pattern, sharp and capable but selective with his energy, would follow him into adult life.

His career has been one of constant reinvention, something he's quietly proud of. "That's what I value most," he says. "Not the money, not the sales. It's the fact I've reinvented myself, again and again."

He started his early career joining the Yellow Pages graduate scheme, a role that gave him rigorous training, experience, and a taste for big business. From there, he moved into the world of exhibitions. This work saw him travel far and wide. In the mid-90s, he was in Moscow, setting up a business at a time when Russia was still opening itself up to the world.

Later, he travelled to Shanghai, helping to build new ventures as China's economy exploded. "It was incredible," he reflects. "You'd be sitting in a room with people from completely different worlds, trying to build something that had never been done before. That shaped me."

Those experiences eventually led him back to the UK, where he took on the NEC Group and transformed it into more than just a venue business. For Paul, it wasn't about running events; it was about connecting everything around them: hospitality, real estate, data, and entertainment. "It had to be bigger than just the shows. It was about the whole experience."

The thread running through all of Paul's experiences, though he didn't have a name for it at the time, was undiagnosed ADHD. Untamed, but always there: His ability to think fast and strategically, to 'run the film' of a meeting in his head long before anyone else had caught up, to see the end game while others were still stuck in the detail. These traits fuelled his success but also caused frustration. Without the understanding or language for ADHD, he hadn't yet learned how to harness them.

"It used to drive me mad in meetings," he says. "I'd be at the end within ten minutes and everyone else was still on the set-up. With meds now, I can be more patient. I can sit through it without checking out."

Paul is honest about the contradictions he experiences with his ADHD explaining that the things that drive him are also the things that exhaust him. He feels his greatest strength is his ability to juggle multiple ideas in his head and navigate between them with ease, identifying opportunities and progressing them all.

On the flip side, his greatest challenge, without doubt, is that inner critic telling him nothing he does is ever good enough. "It's relentless but it drives me." Reflecting on whether he'd change anything about his ADHD, whilst his diagnosis is still new and he's still getting to grips with it, he shares that the ability to just think about one thing at a time would be nice, but that on the whole, ADHD is what makes him who he is.

When thinking about the people closest to him, both at work and at home, he acknowledges that on both sides, he can probably be quite frustrating. "My wife has sometimes struggled with my ADHD diagnosis, but she is the real superstar of this story. She has lived with my behaviour, work life obsession, and throughout held our family together, bringing up 3 wonderful kids and enabled me to go on and realise the things we have. That takes proper grit.'

Paul doesn't hesitate with his advice to newly diagnosed ADHD people thinking of leaping into business or self-employment: "What are you doing sitting around? Get out there and make it happen. Back yourself. Winners are just losers who tried one more time." To himself, the young boy who was capable, but restless and unfocused, he has tremendous empathy "What's going on in your head is absolutely fine."

For all the success Paul has had, the global projects, big deals and billion-pound sales, he always returns to the meaning of it all. There is no time in a boardroom or completing a deal that will ever compare to the day he was awarded his CBE at Buckingham Palace.

"My parents came here with nothing and worked their hearts out. That was for them. It validated everything they sacrificed. That meant more than all the other stuff put together."

Whilst his diagnosis has helped him understand himself better, his restless energy, the need for reinvention and the determination to push further, it doesn't define him. The inner critic that's continually told him nothing he's done is good enough is becoming quieter and he can now finally meet that voice with a confident acceptance of "This is who I am."

Website: www.themarque.com/profile/paul-thandi
LinkedIn: @paul-thandi-cbe-dl-a43a82b

Sonia Ponzo

Co-Founder & CEO at Outset Wellness

"If we can change just one person's life for the better, then this business is a success."

That's the mantra Sonia carried with her when she stepped into entrepreneurship after years in the corporate and academic world. It was never about titles or money in the bank. For her, success meant impact. And when the first Outset Wellness user told her they couldn't imagine life without the app, she knew she'd achieved exactly that.

Sonia Ponzo, originally from Italy, is the CEO and founder of Outset Wellness, a digital health company she created with her partner, Nick, and close friend, Davide. Outset is an ADHD-friendly app that makes movement possible on the days when follow-through feels hardest. It adapts to calendars and weather to strip away decision fatigue, then uses a growing digital garden to make progress visible without guilt or streaks.

Alongside this, Outset offers social support, matching people with others on similar schedules so they can encourage each other and providing a community space where wins and challenges can be shared, making movement feel less isolating and more achievable.

What began as Sonia's attempt to manage her own energy and burnout quickly revealed itself to be something more: a product built, almost by accident, for people like her.

Sonia's story is one of relentless curiosity and drive. A life shaped by both chaos and innovation, of turning struggle into something meaningful. Or, as Nick puts it, "A rocket. She's fast, unstoppable, propelled forward whether you're ready or not."

As a child, her ADHD didn't show up in poor grades but in restlessness. She excelled academically but couldn't be still. At just two years old she was hospitalised after weeks of no sleep and severe headaches. Doctors ran tests, prescribed sedatives—which only made her more hyper and finally sent her mum away with little more than, 'She's hyperactive. Let her run around'.

Her mum and grandparents raised her with patience, feeding her curiosity instead of shutting her down. When she couldn't nap at nursery, teachers built a little "club" to keep her occupied with activities while others slept. By the time she started school she could already read and write and spent much of her first year in the corner with books while her classmates learned the basics.

By 6 years old, she was thriving, her energy channelled into projects that mattered to her. Environmental causes, recycling drives, later politics, and school representation. At home, life was tough. Money was scarce after her parents split and she and her mum shared bunk beds in her grandparents' house before moving to a tiny flat where Sonia slept in the living room. Her mum, juggling multiple jobs, drummed one message into her: education was her ticket out. Sonia listened.

Books became her safe place. She devoured them quickly, playing out stories as films in her head. That curiosity led her to university in Italy and later to the UK, where she studied for a PhD in psychology focused on the mind—body connection and its role in mental health.

But academia soon felt too slow. "The bureaucracy was frustrating. I needed to make an impact faster," she says. She moved into digital health, working her way up from researcher to Head of Research, Director of Science, and eventually VP at a health company providing ADHD and autism assessment services.

Looking back, she can see the pattern she followed. She'd arrive, solve complex problems, build new structures, and then become restless. "I wanted to do the difficult stuff. Once it became maintenance, I lost interest." That need for challenge eventually pulled her into entrepreneurship. Not because she wanted the title of 'founder', but because she saw a problem she couldn't ignore.

Burnout had hit her hard, and exercise was the one constant that helped. But staying consistent was difficult. With Nick's support, she began designing something that removed the barriers: a plan that adapted to her, reduced decision fatigue, made progress visual and social, and turned exercise into something playful. At first, it wasn't framed as an ADHD product. But as the app came to life, it became clear that's exactly what it was. "It made sense," Sonia says. "Motivation, decision fatigue, progress tracking, body doubling—it all speaks to ADHD."

The app's reward system, plants growing in a digital garden with each workout, wasn't just aesthetically pleasing, it gave users tangible progress to see and feel. The social side created accountability, not through PBs or numbers but through comparison of flourishing gardens. And the algorithm adapted to the user, gently encouraging, suggesting workouts based on weather, schedule, and past activity.

Entrepreneurship magnified Sonia's ADHD. Her thoughts became more restless, the noise in her head louder. Bosses and colleagues had hinted at it, but it was only when she was surrounded by ADHD assessments in her VP role that she began to connect the dots. The chaos of building a business pushed her to seek her own diagnosis.

Nick has watched her ADHD show up in ways both brilliant and worrying. "Whatever she does, she goes all in. Business, gardening, finances, cooking, she becomes obsessed until it's done properly." He remembers when Sonia's casual runs turned into marathons of hyperfocus. "She went from short runs to disappearing for hours. One day, she came back delighted she'd run 21k. For her, it was amazing. For me, I'd been pacing the flat, ready to call the police and report her missing," he says in jest.

Food became another fixation. If a takeaway dish had one wrong ingredient, she'd recreate it at home until it was better than the original. And gardening, which started as a digital reward in the app, quickly became an overflowing vegetable patch at home. "That's Sonia," Nick says, "From zero to 100 in no time."

They're often asked if living and working together is difficult, but for them, lockdown was proof they could handle it. After just two months of dating, they chose to move in together when Covid hit. Sonia collected her cat and a suitcase with one week's worth of clothes, and they spent the pandemic side by side, navigating life and business. "We figured everything out quickly," Nick says. "We know how to talk, how to argue, how to build things together."

For Sonia, the hardest part of ADHD is the constant noise. "My brain is never quiet. Sometimes the chaos paralyses me." When her cat died, she remembers it was the only time her mind fell silent. She found it unsettling.

Her greatest strength, though, is determination. "If you put something in front of me, I'll figure it out. My brain feeds on novelty and challenge. That's why being a founder suits me. I do different things every day."

Nick agrees. "She won't leave something until it works. It might not be industry perfect, but it will be good, and she'll understand it. She's relentless." The downside, he adds, is intensity. "She runs at 120% until she breaks. I keep telling her: take a break, look after yourself. You've already proven yourself."

For years, Sonia believed success meant climbing the ladder. When she finally reached the top, she realised nothing really changed. "That freed me. I don't need to keep proving myself." Now success is measured differently. That message from a user, "You've changed my life", meant more than anything she'd achieved in her previous roles.

Nick still calls her a rocket, "Fast, unstoppable, self-propelled." But even rockets need to refuel. Together, Sonia and Nick are learning how to harness ADHD's energy without letting it boil over. Looking back, Sonia says if she could tell her younger self one thing, it would be simple: "It's going to be ok."

Website: www.outsetwellness.com
LinkedIn: @sonia-ponzo
Instagram: @outsetwellness

Maxine Laceby

Co-Founder & CEO at Absolute Collagen

UNSTOPPABLE BY DESIGN

There was nobody there for her. No one to turn to, no one to talk to, no one to feel safe with. And no one to do the things that needed doing. Today, that girl is Maxine Laceby, Co-Founder of Absolute Collagen. No surprise, given her independent childhood, Maxine created a formula, and absolute collagen became the first player and mover in the UK liquid collagen market over a decade ago, with a sachet taken every 1.5 seconds. Known now for her drive and energy, what stands out most about Maxine is how open and authentic she is.

She talks about her life with generosity and without filters, sharing the good, the bad, and the difficult, which she says gave her every strength and quality she has today. Beneath the success is a story of survival and grit. Darcy, her eldest daughter, reflects: "She always trusted me and my sister with everything, because that was her experience growing up. At 12, she gave me a credit card so I could do the food shop. Her ADHD hated food shopping. I don't think that's very normal, but it taught me independence."

Looking back on her childhood, Maxine feels sadness for that little girl, but with time and empathy for everyone around her at the time, she has made peace with it, with herself, and with the people around her at the time.

Her childhood was complicated. Maxine was adopted. Her older brother wasn't. He was the firstborn son, the golden boy and treated like a king. She was the outsider, the 'owl in the nest', and she often wonders if that is due to being adopted or ADHD. Her brother resented having to look after her because their mother, an alcoholic, couldn't. She understood this, and being honest, she resented needing him too. She recalls how they had little money growing up on a council estate, and their mum would wash Maxine's thick curly hair in Fairy Liquid, never a good look! She remembers wearing a school jumper with a grill-burned hole; her attempt to dry-it quickly under the grill had ended in disaster (ADHD brains always find a solution to a problem!) And there was no money to buy a new one. At 13, whilst her mum was working nights, she would be walking the streets.

Yet, despite the chaos, her mum mattered, especially to Maxine. She worked hard, grafted to provide for her family despite her own struggles and 15 years on, Maxine can hold both truths at once: the hardship of being raised by an alcoholic mother, and the compassion of knowing her mum had never been mothered well herself. That empathy allows Maxine to reflect without bitterness. Maxine believes her ADHD gives her the gift of such empathy.

School was also no refuge for Maxine. "I hated school, and school hated me," she shares. Looking back, it's the one part of her childhood she still feels angry about today. ADHD wasn't recognised, and so instead of being supported, she was written off.

"It was a complete waste of time for me," she reflects. Lessons felt alien, teachers didn't understand her, and the sense of being different was reinforced daily. She still thinks the education system is failing many children, with every child being valued on academic ability.

She left at 16, a couple of weeks before she should have, thanks to a broken arm and a plaster cast and never looked back. She recalls having no dreams, no plans, and no encouragement. The only thing that was ever expected of her and voiced on many occasions was, 'don't get pregnant' (Funnily enough, her hair being washed in Fairy Liquid took care of that!) and to earn money for the family. So, she started working.

Initially, she worked in a bookbinding factory, then in cleaning jobs and chambermaid shifts. At that time, there was no plan of a career; she was just trying to make money and survive. Underneath that grit to just get on and do, her ADHD spark was never far away – the spontaneity waiting for something to catch its attention. When a friend suggested touring Europe by car, she was up for it, but with the caveat of them doing it on bikes, and that's what they did for the next ten months. More 'joys' of ADHD, spontaneity and never seeing risk.

When she returned, she carried on job-hopping, trying to earn money, never dreaming of, or wanting a career. Her 20s were spent working and partying hard, whilst exploring her seemingly crazy ideas, one of which was when she was 24 (35 years ago), she came up with the idea for an answer machine intercom but got overwhelmed by the complexities of writing a patent. 30-odd years before the Ring doorbell!

At 49, with a determination to do something for herself, Maxine signed up for a fine art degree at the University of Wolverhampton. She thought she was going to learn about art, but the course ended up teaching her far more about herself.

When she asked for support with her dyslexia, a tutor suggested there was something more. A basic test showed a high likelihood of ADHD. She laughed at the result, calling her high score of 80%+ a 'personal best', and when she told her children, their reply was immediate: 'No shit, Sherlock'. At the time, the cost for assessment and formal diagnosis was out of reach, so she carried that knowledge quietly, but it stayed with her. Years later, with Absolute Collagen growing fast and her profile rising, she realised she needed that official diagnosis to be credible. Either she proved it, or she stopped talking about it.

When the confirmation finally came three years ago, she felt both relief and anger: relief at having an explanation, and anger that she had spent so much of her life misunderstanding herself and her behaviours.

That moment of self-understanding was deeply connected to her fine art project, Dare to Go Bare, which had already started peeling back the layers. For four months, she stripped away her armour, her mask, cutting her hair short, going make-up free and wearing plain, ill-fitting, and oversized clothes. A yellow Post-it note she had written for herself and placed on her mirror read: You are enough. A reminder, an affirmation, and a promise to herself.

It was the beginning of a new relationship with herself, one that gave her the courage to do something different and take a wellness lifestyle choice into an untapped market that would change the landscape forever.

Around the time she was doing her Dare to Bare project, she committed to focusing on her health inside and out. She'd seen that bone broth was all the rage in America, and so she began experimenting for herself. She felt incredible, but more, her friends noticed something different, a glow that wasn't there before. She became obsessed, classic ADHD hyperfocus kicked in. She phoned professors, scientists, and food standards officials, determined to learn everything she could. Her friends wanted a piece of it, and before she knew it, she was making broth for herself and her friends and her family. Her eldest daughter, who by some divine twist of fate had at the last minute switched her university course from psychology to food science, insisted on testing the product her Mum had been making, saying in jest, "Let me test it in the lab before you kill someone!". This testing revealed that the jelly that formed on top was collagen. That discovery became the seed that grew into Absolute Collagen. Darcy shares: "She's like a dog with a bone. Once she has something in her head, she's not ready to let it go. That's why Absolute Collagen exists."

From her kitchen to the sachets available to buy today, Maxine brought a brand-new concept to market. She was the first player and mover in the UK liquid collagen space, building a £30 million business from scratch. But what mattered to her wasn't just the product; it was the price.

Competitors and even journalists keen to know more about her and the business told her she could charge more. Private equity voices questioned her. But Maxine went inward and asked herself one question: Could my mum, with the little she had, have afforded this? That question became her compass. She remembered being six, walking the aisles of the department stores with her mum, watching other women buy lipsticks that her mum would never have been able to afford. Absolute Collagen would never replicate that exclusion. "For me, those absoluters (as they call themselves) represent my mum at different decades of her life", she says. "She had nothing, she couldn't afford anything, and I will never let her down, ever. So, I guess, my product is really about empowerment."

Darcy adds: "I don't think she could ever do something without real purpose and meaning. Everything she's ever done is for me and my sister."

She describes her ADHD as both rocket fuel and a curse. Hyperfocus, creativity, empathy and emotional intelligence have all been undeniable strengths for her. But the other side — the risky behaviour, impulsivity, and spending — has been more challenging. "Many years ago, I was given the nickname Spendy Spice," she jokes. "I can make money, But I'm also very aware I'm really good at spending it, one in every colour!" Again, a classic ADHD trait.

Darcy laughs about her mum's extremes: two matcha makers, two pairs of cycling shoes, endless kit for hobbies she'll dive into then abandon. "She doesn't do anything by halves, whether it's business or hobbies, it's always full tilt."

She's open about the darker parts that her ADHD has led her to as well. She's struggled with addiction, spent time in rehab and, at times, hit low-lows and felt near-suicidal. She shares that she hasn't drunk for over a decade but also acknowledges it hasn't been easy. "Even those things, those darker days, have gone on to make me the person I am today".

Through it all, she has always backed herself. When Absolute Collagen began, she went all in, remortgaging the house, selling jewellery and even her motorbike. But she has learned with maturity to consider the consequences of any risk. Before she took the leap with Absolute Collagen, she sat her daughters down and laid out the risk: if it failed, they would have to sell the house and buy a smaller one. They understood and agreed, and that gave her permission to go for it.

For Maxine, their support mattered more than anything. Her relationship with her girls and her commitment to them has been at the heart of every decision she has ever made. Darcy puts it simply: "Everything she does is for us, even when I think she's bonkers. People believe in her because she's passionate and genuine. That's what makes her different."

Now at 59, Maxine is clear. She wouldn't change her past, even the darkest parts. "I like who I am today, I get me, and I'm fully aware I am who I am today because of everything I've ever experienced. The good, the bad and the damn ugly."

Her advice to anyone newly diagnosed is simple: give yourself time. Sit with it. Get to understand it, get to understand you, make peace with it, mourn the things that haven't worked, embrace the things that have, and truly fall in love with yourself. All of you.

If you have an idea for a new business or a new venture, don't stare at the overwhelming big picture; just take the next step. And don't sit on it forever. Take the risk, just make sure you think through the consequences, and you can live with those consequences if it doesn't work out.

And to the younger Maxine, the adopted girl who felt unwanted, who thought she was the stain in the council house? She wouldn't say a word. "I wouldn't change any of it. Even the worst bits made me who I am. I'd just tell her, you're exactly where you're supposed to be." Darcy's words close the loop: "She always says it's just little old me doing my thing," but for Darcy, her mum is living proof you can turn that grit into something amazing.

Website: www.absolutecollagen.com
LinkedIn: @maxinelaceby
Instagram: @maxinelaceby

CHAPTER 2
The Practitioners & Coaches*

*Here we meet the people working on the ground, side by side with others, to create real and lasting change. They are coaches, therapists, educators, and mentors who bring their lived experience and professional skills together to help others thrive. Their work is deeply personal, and their impact is often life-changing.

Amy Polly

Chief Mindfulness Rebel at Funfulness® Inc |
Creative Wellbeing Lead at ADHD 360 |
TEDx and International Speaker

Amy Polly is now the Creative Wellbeing Lead at ADHD 360, but before joining, she founded Funfulness Inc, a business built around teaching mindfulness in a way that works for neurodivergent people. She explains, "I don't teach it in the traditional sense. I make it fun, Funfulness. It strips away all the 'shoulds' and makes mindfulness accessible, inclusive and human."

Her early life was shaped by the closeness of her family. "Even though there were tough times, I had a lovely childhood," she says. Her granddad's long-term alcohol addiction created strain at home, but Amy found comfort and safety in her parents, and her Nanny (Grandmother), who she describes as 'like a second mum'. She was always the joker, quick to make people laugh, and she remembers being happiest in the garden with her grandparents or hanging out with her brother.

Reflecting on her school days, she always felt it was something she had to endure rather than enjoy. Amy recalls not having close friends during that time, which upset her mum when she mentioned it years later. But, as Amy told her, "Why did I need friends at school when I had you?" She was a busy girl, filling her time with Air Cadets, netball, and hockey. "I've always felt different. I am, and always was, loud, excitable, energetic, and silly," she says. "I wasn't good at reading social cues or fitting in. Everyone else bought the same tracksuit. I bought a luminous orange Adidas one because it made me happy."

When she appeared on the ADHD Beyond the Label TV show, she found her old school reports, which gave some context to her early years. Reading them back with the knowledge of her ADHD, in hindsight they clearly ticked off almost every ADHD checklist. On the show Phil Anderton, her ADHD 360 boss, and co-host of the show, remarked, "It's like reading the DSM-5!". Teachers wrote that her 'work was always late, had poor detail, she was disruptive but lively'. Her oral work was strong, and exams were passable, but coursework was always a struggle.

"I knew I wasn't stupid. I just couldn't always apply myself." Despite bullying and bad decisions made in attempts to fit in, she made her parents proud, scraped by with mostly B's and C's and moved onto the next chapter of her life.

Motherhood was the catalyst for her ADHD diagnosis. She loved being pregnant but after her son was born, she was overwhelmed with anxiety. "I was crippled. I couldn't leave the house, had heart palpitations and shortness of breath. Looking back, I know I was doing well as a mum, but at the time I felt like I wasn't."

Two years later, after recognising she still didn't feel right, she spoke to her GP. "She didn't mention all the things I'd read about in my Dr Google search, but she did mention ADHD." She was referred on the Right to Choose pathway to a company then unknown to her, and after an initial assessment, three months later in late 2021, she received her formal diagnosis. "That was emotional. It answered so many questions. The birth of my son was the catalyst. Before him, I only had myself to manage. Add in hormones, the work juggle, and motherhood, and things just fell apart. That's what led me to seek help."

She has since shared her story on BBC News to raise awareness so people have the knowledge and understanding before reaching that point, particularly for women who may only recognise ADHD traits in themselves in moments of crisis.

Her greatest entrepreneurial success is, without doubt, creating Funfulness Inc. Mindfulness, she says, changed her life in so many ways: helping her mum through depression, her Nanny through dementia, and supporting herself through the early years of motherhood. She wanted to strip mindfulness of the barriers, the expectation to sit still, be calm and be quiet, which "doesn't work for everyone, especially neurodivergent people," she explains. Her TEDx talk on Funfulness became a standout moment, a proud one, and clearly affirmed that her approach resonated significantly with an audience far and wide.

Amy describes her ADHD as "an exciting, hilarious, fucking nightmare". She rejects labels of either 'superpower' or 'disability', instead calling it a combination of both. "With support, it can feel like a superpower. Without it, it can be debilitating." Creativity, crisis management and supporting others are among her strengths. On the opposite side, concentration, emotional regulation, and admin tasks remain challenging. "With compassion and support, struggles can be managed, but they never completely disappear."

Others often describe her as joyful, kind, and compassionate, though she admits she's known for her clumsiness. At home, breaking or spilling something is jokingly referred to as 'doing an Amy Polly'. She acknowledges her whirlwind style but stresses, "I always get the job done. The process might look chaotic, but the outcome is always solid."

Her time management is the thing she would most like to change. Her approach is zigzag when she wishes it could be a straight line. Clutter also causes tension. "I don't notice mess until it overwhelms me. Then I feel shame about inviting people over. That probably affects me the most."

At the same time, she credits ADHD for shaping her confidence. She thrives on adrenaline and dopamine, and public speaking brings her joy rather than fear. Setting up Funfulness Inc and becoming her own boss gave her freedom and creativity, but it also caused stress and strain. "The admin, the money management, the prioritising — it was overwhelming. That's why I'm so passionate about neuroinclusive workplaces. Many ADHD entrepreneurs say they can't work for others, but often that's because workplaces aren't inclusive. With trust, flexibility and autonomy, people with ADHD could thrive in employment too."

When asked what part of her positive ADHD traits Amy would amplify, she didn't choose more for herself but instead wished she could impart it to others. She shares that if she could gift non-ADHDers with the "confidence that I feel when I stand on stage, that confidence because of my ADHD, I would. To give people who think 'I could never do that' the ability to have self-belief."

Late diagnosis and moving into your calling is hard, but Amy has sound advice for those in that position. "Talk to yourself as you would your best friend. You're not stupid or broken." She believes in showing yourself compassion, acknowledging how you feel, validating your emotions rather than bottling them up, and surrounding yourself with a trusted support network you can lean on and give back to.

112

If she could go back and talk to her teenage self, her message would be simple: "Don't put so much weight on finding a romantic relationship. Don't lose yourself to be loved or accepted. Don't do stupid things for validation. Have the confidence to walk away. Don't compromise who you are."

In the end, Amy's ADHD is exactly what makes her who she is: creative, resilient, kind, and always ready with an infectious laugh that makes everything feel lighter.

Website: www.amypolly.com
LinkedIn: @amypolly
Instagram: @thisisamypolly

Adam Smith

Director at A-Game Consultancy

The blackboard blurred in front of him. Adam would glance up, find his place, scribble fast to keep up and then stare down at writing he couldn't even read. By the time he looked back up, he'd lost his place again. The frustration was unbearable.

Adam Smith, that distracted and restless boy, is now the Director and Founder of A-Game Consultancy, a coaching practice built on mindset, nutrition, fitness, retreats, and transformation. His work has reached companies like Amazon and Dell, sold out retreats and supported hundreds of clients. But beyond the numbers, Adam has built something rarer: spaces where people, especially men, feel safe enough to talk about what they've carried for decades, and start to let it go.

He grew up as a lively, outdoorsy child who thrived on activity, but the classroom was always a battleground. What came easily to others rarely stuck for him, and the harder he tried, the more frustrated he became. "School was awful, very challenging," Adam said. "I liked PE, and I loved playtime and lunchtime, but the classroom side was horrendous. It wasn't that I didn't like learning, it was that I couldn't retain information the same way other people could."

Teachers often described him as funny and polite, but behind the jokes, he couldn't keep up. His ADHD and dyspraxia went undiagnosed for years. Even as a child, he was tuned into people in a way others weren't, noticing how teachers yelled and how children responded. But fascination with people didn't translate into grades. Where friends did well, Adam didn't, leaving him feeling 'less than'. Through determination, he became captain of the football team and represented the county, but inside, he still felt misunderstood, angry, and confused.

Adam was eventually diagnosed with both dyspraxia and ADHD in his teens, though the two experiences couldn't have felt more different. The dyspraxia was clear. "At 14 or 15 I was asked to colour in and cut paper with scissors. I felt humiliated. But they told my mum straight away, 'he's definitely got dyspraxia'." ADHD was much hazier. A support teacher recognised his struggles weren't about intelligence, but about keeping up, which led to an assessment at a clinic in Harrogate. "I reluctantly got tested and was diagnosed," Adam said, "but it didn't give me the validation I'd hoped for." He says he'd like a full assessment now, as an adult, to get the clarity he didn't as a child.

Although some teachers offered support post-diagnosis, Adam rejected it. "I felt embarrassed and ashamed," he said. The stigma was crushing. One teacher told him he had 'sheep shit for brains', and more often than not, he spent lessons in the corridor, sent out for misbehaving. His school also had a unit known as L9, for children needing extra support or with behaviour issues. Adam remembers the humiliation of being regularly singled out because the other children would weaponise it. "At breaktimes, I'd head to the playground to play football with the cool kids, and they'd make jibes about me being sent to L9. It just made me angrier, and resistant to help."

By Year 10 he had mentally checked out. "I thought, right, I'll just work for my dad. He had a successful plumbing and heating business. I saw the nice cars and thought I'd take over. I didn't have a clue what it actually involved." He left school with 3 GCSEs. "The message was clear: without 5 GCSEs, you were a failure. It crushed my self-esteem." With little direction, he stepped into his dad's trade.

Plumbing proved unbearable. "6ft 4", 17 stone, dyspraxic, terrified of heights and trying to bend pipes within a millimetre? I hated every second." He left and fell into hospitality, where he stayed for 14 years. It was long hours, poor pay, and an endless grind. "I didn't value the transferable skills. All I felt was misery."

By his late twenties, everything unravelled. A relationship ended, family members died, and his mental health collapsed. "One night I drank 8 beers at a wake, got in my car, and drove at 100mph towards a bridge intending to end my life. My mum called to say I'd left my wallet at home. That phone call saved me. I slammed the brakes, the car spun out, and I sobbed for hours. That was rock bottom."

From there, he rebuilt: 5 years sober, 30kg lighter, in a healthy relationship, and finally out of hospitality. During lockdown, he set up his coaching practice. His proudest entrepreneurial success isn't revenue but scale. "Most coaches burn out because they are the business. I realised people weren't reaching out because they wanted me personally; they wanted the solutions in my content. So, I created a system where I handle the sales call, then match the client to one of our contracted coaches. Clients still see me in group sessions, but they get consistent coaching from others. It freed up my diary and tripled our sales in a quarter. The coaches win, the clients win and the business wins."

Among the initiatives he's built, the men's retreats stand out most. "Society says men don't talk, but they do, when they feel safe. At our retreats, men open up about trauma they've carried for decades. Seeing breakthroughs like that, in a safe space, is incredible. It's transformational work I'm most proud of."

Adam calls his ADHD "exhausting and amazing." Later DNA results backed up what he already knew deep down. "My need for dopamine is sky high, but my brain's reception for it is very low." It leaves him crashing in the afternoons, heavy with fatigue, yet when the hyperfocus switch flips, he becomes unstoppable. In a burst of focus, he can do in three hours what others might take three days to complete. "Once, on a two-hour flight, I wrote 22 LinkedIn posts."

It shows up just as vividly in everyday life. "My business partner makes a cup of tea step by step. I go in to make tea, see the washing, put the kettle on, decide I need a wee, the doorbell goes... and still no cup of tea. That's ADHD."

The same traits that make Adam brilliant can also trip him up. "I bought clothes before the holiday. They didn't fit. I needed to send them back, but I didn't get enough dopamine from repackaging and posting them. I avoided it, missed the deadline, and lost £150." He thinks this is definitely one of the things that his partner finds hardest about his ADHD, that, and his emotional reactions. "But she also sees my empathy and strengths." His mum saw the challenging side of him in his childhood, but he shares "now she calls me for advice." He describes his ADHD is a blessing, and a curse for those around him, but that mix is what makes him who he is.

Adam is also known for his openness, especially online. "People say, 'Oh my God, that's me.' It's never about me; it's about them seeing themselves in my words. Vulnerability is often misunderstood. I've learned that if you tell your story first, no one can use it against you. That's how I see it, disarming any bullshit that might come my way."

Would he change anything about ADHD? "No. You can't have the good without the bad. Everything has been a lesson and made me stronger." If anything, he'd amplify one trait. "The hyperfocus. If I could bottle that up and sell it, it'd be worth millions."

His advice to others starting out with ADHD is simple. "Get a coach. Do the deep inner work, not just surface stuff. Otherwise, you'll sabotage yourself. And keep it simple. Don't try to do everything at once. Break it into small steps. Buy the trainers. Walk 100 yards. Build-up. I use a simple notes app and green ticks for tasks. That's it."

Asked what he'd say to his 14-year-old self, Adam is clear: "You're going to be ok, mate. Don't be so hard on yourself. The fear of what was to come was worse than the reality. Someone putting their arm around me then, and saying, 'you are enough' would have helped."

He remembers an exercise he did with a photo of his younger self. "I said, 'You poor little sod' and I cried harder than I ever have. Hours of release. I realised whenever I criticise myself now, I'm criticising that little boy. That reframed everything for me."
Adam's journey doesn't tidy itself into neat boxes; it is messy, and at times painful, yet threaded with grit, humour, and an ability to turn setbacks into fuel. He carries the words of teachers who dismissed

him, but he's also built something no exam or grade could ever measure.

"I look back at that boy who thought he was stupid, in the school corridor, who wanted the bell to go so he could escape. If I could show him the life we've built now, he wouldn't believe it. And that's the point, you never really know what's possible until you back yourself."

Website: agameconsultancy.com
LinkedIn: @adam-smith-high-performance-coach
Instagram: @adamsmith_agame

Ella McCrystal

Trauma Expert & Psychotherapist |
The New Mind Podcast Host

Secrets defined Ella McCrystal's childhood. Some were imposed on her, others she created for herself. She learned early to lie, to hide things in her mattress, to carry shame that wasn't hers. By the age of seven, her world had fractured.

At eleven, she disclosed what was happening at home: her dad had sexually abused her. Years later, he would be arrested, charged, and sent to prison for this, but for Ella, that blend of trauma together with her undiagnosed ADHD would become the backdrop for everything that followed.

Today, Ella is a psychotherapist, trauma expert, and clinic owner. She has developed her own therapeutic method; one she now trains others in, particularly powerful for people with ADHD and autism. "There's so much trauma attached to that," she says. "Whenever I do an ADHD podcast, my inbox is so full that I can't cope with it."

Before the fractures, Ella remembers herself as imaginative and obsessive. "If I loved something, I'd become quite obsessed with it quickly. I had an obsession with butterflies that stayed with me for a long time."

But at school, she was already living a double life. "I would dissociate from what was difficult at home, and then go to school, and act as though nothing had happened. But at school, I was easily distracted. I was a bit mouthy, but also felt like a John Wayne character; if anybody was getting picked on, it would be me who stepped in. I always had that sense of justice, even as a kid."

That justice rarely extended to herself. "If someone was picking on me, I didn't have the same voice. You feel like you're not enough, or too much, so your sense of justice for yourself is diluted."

Her adolescence was marked by secrecy and self-soothing. "There was always a level of addiction for me: food, alcohol, money, work, spending." At 13 she worked in a cake shop and recalls taking all the left-over cakes home and eating them. "There was no off switch." Schoolwork followed the same cycle: paralysis, then last-minute sprints. "Unless I am in an emergency situation, I can't get started. That's always been the case."

Looking back, she sees ADHD in every corner: obsessions, risk-taking, extremes. When tested later, her childhood ADHD score was 87 out of 90. "One of the highest my assessor had ever seen."

When she was 16, her dad was released from prison. Her mum brought him back into the family home. For Ella, it was a second betrayal that cut even deeper than the first. "There was no safeguarding. My mum's primary goal was to keep the family together. So, I moved out." Leaving home at sixteen forced Ella into survival mode. She carried addictions into her twenties, drinking, bingeing, and overspending, alongside the continued chaos of undiagnosed ADHD. Conventional jobs never lasted. "I couldn't maintain a job because I was always late or didn't turn up. It was chaos again."

Instead, she built her own businesses: singing, entertainment, and children's parties. Each one succeeded, until she burned out. She shares that she could never stay at one pace. Initially, it would be full speed ahead, and then it would be gone completely – interest, motivation, and resources to carry on.

It wasn't until years later, during a neurodiversity training course, that ADHD entered the frame. "The tutor pulled me over at the end and said, 'do you realise when you're listening, you don't stop moving, but when you're talking, you hold yourself really well, almost like a different character? Have you ever thought you might have ADHD?'."

At first, she laughed. "I thought, there's absolutely no way. Our understanding of ADHD was naughty little boys, not someone like me." But over time, she began to see how it explained her lifelong patterns: nail biting, binge eating, anorexia, addiction, and self-harm obsessions.

Two years later, she sought a formal assessment. Without family members to provide history, she leaned on school reports, and a close friend. The results were clear. "The assessor said, 'Look, you're definitely ADHD'. I still questioned it. I asked, 'what about the childhood sexual abuse?'. She said she thought the reason I've survived it so well is because of the resilience I've got with ADHD. It enabled me to have a separate part that just got into action during the chaos."

The diagnosis brought relief, but also denial. "I still struggle to believe I have it. Sometimes I question, is this neurodevelopmental ADHD, or acquired because of trauma? I gaslight myself the same way my clients do."

Psychotherapy was the turning point for her. An interest in medical hypnosis led to a five-year training course. She went straight into private practice, then joined the Northampton Clinic, the very place she had once dreamed of working, eventually buying the business and the building itself whilst raising her young daughter. "That was probably my biggest entrepreneurial success. I'd always said I wanted my own clinic, a team working together across disciplines. And I did it. I bought the building; I built the business."

She also self-published a book and gave a TEDx talk. But she downplays them. "I wasn't particularly proud of it. I didn't think I did that well. I never feel good enough." Her eyes are fixed on what comes next: a training school, an app, and a supplement brand. "That will be amazing. But even then, I'll probably say it's not enough."

Ella credits ADHD with her determination, grit, and creativity. "Everything I've done that's been an achievement starts with a single idea. I become obsessed with it, excited by it, and it manifests into something successful."

She also reframes masking as a tool. "What other people call being a chameleon in a negative sense is one of my greatest strengths. If I see 50 people a week, I have to be able to move and manoeuvre. My ability to blend to each person is what makes me a good therapist."

But the challenges are heavy. "I could be so excited by life, but then if I stop, it doesn't take long for the engine to slow down and completely stop. For me, it goes into quite a heavy, dark cloud. I have suicidal ideations. If I create space, and stillness, my nervous system says, 'Do you even want to be alive?'."

Her way through is to regulate. "I bilaterally tap and do breathwork for two minutes. I try to see the thought as the inner child who never felt loved and send that part compassion instead of hatred. For me, it works within ten minutes."

She explains that the people around her can see the contradictions clearly. Colleagues see her as 'scatty, unorganised, terrible at admin, but with incredible interpersonal skills' – my superpower." At home, her daughter laughs with her about ADHD quirks but has also seen the emotional rollercoaster. Friends often don't believe she has ADHD at all because she masks so well.

Ella herself admits she keeps people at arm's length. "I don't have a mum, dad, brother, or sister around me. All my friendships from back then are entwined with the family system and the abuse, so I'm dissociated from them. It's kind of me, myself, and I. Hyper-independence. That's what it is."

She knows it has a cost. "There are people who love me and want to be let in, but I am too busy. I don't let people get close. People say the way I work isn't healthy, but if I stop, that's when I'm unhealthiest." For much of her life, Ella's identity was defined by her childhood trauma. "Everything, my whole life, was put on to being a figure of sexual abuse. When I got the ADHD diagnosis, I took a sigh of relief. This isn't all about abuse. There's another part of me."

ADHD has also connected her to new opportunities and people she describes as phenomenal. Her advice to others is simple. "Grit and determination are everything. If I've said I'm going to do something, it happens. That determination is what carries me through, even when I never feel it's enough."

Ella reflects a lot on her younger self. It's how she's learned to work through the trauma. She is clear on what she would say to herself, if she could go back: "I feel so sorry for that little girl that wasn't allowed to be upset, wasn't allowed to have those feelings. When we get older, we must show the love, and compassion to those parts that we were never given, because otherwise we're just going to stay in this perpetual cycle, which doesn't serve us."

And in showing compassion to that little girl, Ella has also shown countless others what is possible: that survival can become strength, that silence can give way to voice, and that healing is never just for yourself, it ripples outward.

Website: ellamccrystal.com
LinkedIn: @ella-mccrystal-3ab0a137
Instagram: @ellamccrystal

Alex Campbell

Co-Founder & Director Gold Mind Academy |
Founder ADHD Alex | ADHD Coach | Keynote Speaker

At eleven years old, Alex was already hustling. Whilst other children were swapping football stickers, he was raiding the cupboards at school, and at home for anything he could sell at the local car boot sale. "Nothing was going back. Partly because I just didn't want to put it back where I'd found it, that would be so boring. I was so driven. I'd clear the entire car boot. That was just the ADHD brain looking for the dopamine hit."

That same restless drive has never really left him. Today, Alex Campbell is a psychotherapist, ADHD coach, keynote speaker, and co-founder of Gold Mind Academy, an ICF-accredited ADHD coach training company. He's also the co-author of 'ADHD: Now What? How ADHD Coaching can help you take back your power" and his professional life is still shaped by the same energy that made him that kid at the car boot sale. Only now, it's channelled into creating safe spaces for others to understand themselves.

Alex grew up in a time when ADHD was barely recognised in the UK. Back in 1990, he was one of the first 40 children to be diagnosed and treated in the UK. "I was the only kid with ADHD at school, at cubs, at anything I did. I was that kid, bouncing off the walls, and never shutting up."

From the age of 7, he went to boarding school. He recognises that his privilege gave him access to one of the only schools in the country with teachers trained in ADHD, but even then, understanding was still limited. "What was missing for me was all the stuff around regulation. The focus then was just: get the kids in school, get them the grades. There was nothing about socialisation. I have no friends from school. Zero."

The school years were also laced with punishment. "We were in the final year of the cane. Physical punishment really messed with my nervous system, and so much of my behaviour was seen as bad behaviour rather than dysregulation. 'Alex is acting out' rather than Alex is overwhelmed."

Looking back now, he can see the entrepreneurial spark, and leadership that were hidden at the time. "Now I can see the brilliance. Back then, it was buried in shame."

Reflecting on his upbringing, Alex also suspects both of his parents may be ADHD, and that likely shaped some of their parenting. His father, a successful lawyer, poured himself into work but was quite absent. "When a parent doesn't understand their neurological differences, it massively influences how you raise your kids. My ability was challenging for my parents. I think they saw things in me they never got to realise for themselves."

As a teenager, Alex discovered the arts gave him refuge. At age 16, he was already working on television, inspired by Abby Collins, the UK's only female stunt coordinator. Soon he was racking up credits on The Royal, Heartbeat, Bond, and Bridget Jones.

He deliberately avoided film school, opting for Staffordshire University instead. "University was the first place I found friends. I tested those friendships hard, but they stuck. For the first time, I felt genuinely wanted."
It was also where his academic story flipped. After years of underperformance, he graduated with First Class Honours and received the Dean's Award for highest achievement. "How do you

go from Cs and Ds at GCSE to that? It was the environment. It was doing something I loved. That was the difference."

Before university, he took 18 months to explore the world, travelling to New Zealand, Australia, Singapore, Ghana, and Camp America. The experience transformed him. "My family were shocked at the Alex who came back. I'd grown up. Travelling gave me independence. It also gave me danger, like when a train got hijacked in Ghana. My ADHD brain kept me safe. The speed at which I can pick up on danger, that neuroception, it's part of who I am."

After university, Alex's career in the film industry took off. It was exhilarating, chaotic, and full of neurodivergent people. But it was also unsustainable. "I was heading to burnout faster, and harder, chasing dopamine like it was going out of fashion. I self-medicated with drugs like everyone around me. Then I burnt out."

The turning point came at a wrap party. "I looked at people in positions I thought I wanted and thought, 'I don't want that to be me'. I want a family, kids. I'm not heading in that direction." Leaving film triggered what he calls his wilderness year. His identity was consumed by work. "I couldn't even watch TV or movies because I couldn't bear not seeing my name in the credits."

It was after burning out of film that ADHD came back into focus. While retraining in psychotherapy, Alex thrived in the experiential elements but kept failing essays. A retired psychotherapist stepped in to help him decode his writing, peeling apart what he was trying to say. Even with that support, the struggle was still there. A fellow student quietly suggested it might be ADHD and at first, he dismissed it, not wanting to reopen that particular can of worms.

Later, he took an online self-assessment, which suggested he might have ADHD, no surprises there, and he was fast-tracked through the Ealing crisis team and given medication. Starting treatment, and getting a coach transformed things, and the change he felt was immediate. "I literally went from failing my papers to getting distinctions overnight. That was the power of acknowledging it was ADHD."

Alex speaks about his strengths with conviction, often borrowing the language of the VIA strengths framework he uses with clients. "Empathy. The speed I pick up on nuance. I can hold perspective in high-emotion spaces. Creativity, not just in the artistic sense, but knowing what brilliance looks like, and going for it. I create safe spaces where people feel seen."

But there are shadows too. "Emotional regulation, especially as a parent. I love my work, but that means I use up all my energy. Then I walk into the house depleted, and that's when I lose it.

Neurotypicals connect to importance — they stop and pick things up tomorrow. My brain connects to interest — I have to finish or I'll lose it. That's when frustration and shouting at the kids happens." If asked whether he'd change anything, his answer depends on which version of him he answers from. "Old Alex would have said: change my strong emotions. Current Alex says: It's not about changing me, it's about recognising the work ADHD demands of me. Emotional regulation is my challenge, but it's also part of me."

After retraining, Alex co-founded Gold Mind Academy with his business partner, Katie Friedman. Their partnership has been the cornerstone of his entrepreneurial success. "So many ADHD entrepreneurs go it alone. We have a high need for connection. If you don't get that need met, you'll chase dopamine, and you'll fuck it. Finding Katie changed everything."

Their brains complement each other: she holds strategy, he thrives in operations. "When you team up with someone who shares your ADHD but has different interests, it's magic. It's when both of you can sit in your brilliance without comparison. That's what keeps partnerships alive."

Together they've built a programme known for weaving identity into the heart of ADHD coaching. "It's not about Pomodoro timers or task lists. It's about knowing yourself and doing you with purpose. That's the difference we teach."

Alex shares that his colleagues would describe him as creative, quick, and sometimes intense. Katie reminds him constantly of his empathy, and emotional intelligence. His children? "They'd probably say I'm fun but distracted. Amazing but frustrating."

Alex doesn't hold back on the realities either. "Prioritise your wellbeing. If you don't, you're screwed. Get support. Use Access to Work if you can (in the UK). Don't try to get every duck in a row alone; most of those ducks are boring but vital. Invest in a coach and get a mentor. Recognise that the transition from employment to entrepreneurship is massive. Don't rush it."

He also challenges the familiar ADHD mantra. "Try harder, do more, be better. That's what we've grown up with. It leads to burnout. The work is figuring out how to get interested in what's important, not just what's interesting."

If he could speak to his 15-year-old self, Alex would be gentle. "You're not broken. You're not weird. You have so much potential. All the frustrations weren't in vain; they made you who you are. Well done for surviving without knowing what you now know. None of your childhood is lost, you're reclaiming it now with a more affirming lens. You always sought truth, and now you're closer to it. Make sure you surround yourself with good people."

Alex's story has never been neat. It has been messy, risky, brilliant, and demanding, a life built on constant cycles of risk and renewal. From car boot sales at 11 years old, to blockbuster film sets, from burnout to reinvention, he has continually found a way to transform chaos into purpose. What makes his journey remarkable is not only the successes, but the courage to name the costs, and still stand firmly in the truth that ADHD is not brokenness, it is brilliance lived differently.

Website:	www.goldmindacademy.com
LinkedIn:	@adhdalex
Instagram:	@goldmindcoach

Dr Samantha Hiew

Founder ADHD Girls | Intersectionality & Neurodiversity
Professional Speaker and Consultant | Author

The image of a Phoenix runs through Dr Samantha Hiew's story. Rising, falling, and rising again. She has built a life that speaks to reinvention, resilience, and truth. Today, she is the founder of ADHD Girls, a social impact company with a dual mission: to empower neurodivergent women to thrive, and to elevate understanding of neurodiversity through an intersectional lens. She is also a neurodiversity educator, women's empowerment champion, former scientist, and mother of two.

Her journey has been full of sharp turns, zigzags, and steep climbs, but each one has shaped the determination, purpose, and unapologetic voice she carries now. "The first 30 years of my life were spent experimenting, making a lot of mistakes," she says. "The next 30, which is where I am now, are about making sense of those mistakes, trying not to make them again, and practising discernment."

Growing up in Malaysia as the eldest daughter of five, Samantha quickly became "the second mother." From changing nappies to keeping her siblings in line, responsibility was placed firmly on her shoulders. "My siblings both played with me and also thought of me as a disciplinarian, because I had to keep everyone in check." That early sense of sacrifice, always fixing, helping, making sure everyone else was ok, became second nature.

ADHD showed itself clearly in her energy. "I was very athletic. Hyperactivity manifested itself on the field. At some point, I realised I was running faster than other people, then suddenly I was put into races, then winning them." But puberty slowed her down. Weight gain and poor concentration saw her slipping behind and nearly failing her exams. She remembers pleading with her maths teacher for another chance: "'If you pass me this time, I'll do better next.' The next exam I got 100%, from 39% before. I was confused: how could I nearly fail and then get full marks?"

That contradiction, excelling in bursts but stumbling in routine, became a theme. At sixteen, her biology teacher, Mrs Fun, gave her a new sense of direction. "Understanding the process of how life came to be gave me so much comfort. Around the same time, I was reading stories about cancer survivors who completely reassessed their life priorities, to get a second chance at life... and I was hooked on a purpose... I told myself I was going to cure cancer." With a scholarship, she moved to the UK to pursue cancer research, a dream that unravelled quickly. "The postgraduate science labs were inaccessible for someone who thought the way I did. I never knew what was expected. I was in fight or flight most of the time."

What followed were her "train wreck years": a decade of drinking, travelling, heartbreak and searching for belonging. After her PhD, she left the lab and landed in an existential crisis. "Who was I, if the science lab wasn't my place?" She then experimented with careers in 16 industries, from pharmaceuticals, modelling, writing to medical and healthcare comms, never feeling at home in any of them.

Then came motherhood and that changed everything. "I developed postnatal anxiety and depression. My boss at the time refused my flexible working request. He said, 'If you're not here, nothing happens.' I couldn't leave my baby; I was breastfeeding, anxious and with no family support. I quit."

For years, she tried to be the perfect mother, and even if she loved spending time with her daughter, inside, she knew there was a part of her that was suppressed, and she was deeply unhappy. "You either choose motherhood or a career. I thought, no, I'm not choosing."

When her son was born, she couldn't ignore the call any longer. "I couldn't wait another five or six years to do my own thing. I started ADHD Girls whilst breastfeeding him, writing and creating campaigns during the night feeds. At first, it was just an effort to stay alive in my head. Not for profit, just an urge and a determination to create, a life force I had suppressed."

As the company grew, in her personal life, her marriage was ending. Juggling single parenthood and entrepreneurship was brutal, but creating ADHD Girls gave her a way back to herself. "For so long, I tried to fit into a destiny that wasn't mine. Finally, I was able to be authentic, and life felt fulfilling."

Thinking about her diagnosis, Samantha explains that it came through community. She never fit the stereotype of the "naughty white schoolboy," even if she had been hyperactive as a child and her endless internal chatter was deafening. Motherhood only intensified it. Scrolling through social media one night, she noticed successful women and entrepreneurs talking openly about ADHD.

Until then, she had assumed it was a severe disorder that happened to people who did drugs, attempted suicide, or ended up in prison. Yet here were accomplished business owners and professionals describing their own experiences. Curiosity took hold, and in true ADHD fashion, her hyperfocus switched on. She threw herself into understanding, determined to uncover what ADHD looked like in women.

That curiosity turned into action, and she began interviewing women worldwide, launching the Utopia campaign to explore ADHD across cultures and contexts. "There was a truth about ADHD, and there was this whole other truth about being a woman in today's world.

When these two identities collide, we've had to find our way, masked, camouflaged – it's no surprise we were missed." Her own assessment was deeply painful. "Psychiatrists asked about childhood, about 'bad things' that had to have happened. Afterwards, I thought, what now? After an argument with my ex-husband, for the first time in my life, I thought maybe it would be better if I wasn't here. That shocked me because I had always been resilient. That's when I realised what I was reading was feeding a compulsion."

Hormones magnified everything. "It wasn't just ADHD. It was perimenopause. It was postpartum changes. You can do all the post-traumatic healing in the world, but if your hormones and your internal rhythms aren't aligned, you will struggle to become well. You need to address your physical needs first."

With time, she came to see the duality of her brain. "My attention to detail, ability to spot connections, see patterns, hold the big picture and then run with it, that's my strength." The challenges with AuDHD were equally stark (if not more so). She went through a 7-month ASD assessment process that was deeply painful, where she was gaslit and told it was her trauma, not ASD. But she was suffering from side effects from stimulant medication. "With AuDHD, the regulation zone is narrow. Overstimulation led to mania-like episodes, under-stimulation to rumination."

Switching gears is one of Samantha's hardest challenges. Her pathological demand avoidance (PDA) often feels like a constant battle with herself, knowing what she wants or needs to do, but feeling blocked from doing it. Time blindness adds another layer, creating daily anxiety for her and her children, whilst in relationships, it is often her messiness and emotional intensity that cause the greatest strain.

Yet those closest to her also see her strengths. Her children describe her as brave, sometimes fiery, and deeply spiritual. And at work, she's been called inspiring and validating, someone who has a rare ability to get under people's skin and make them feel truly seen and understood.

Professionally, she points to her DSM-5 criteria through a scientific and intersectional lens programme as a breakthrough and one of her biggest achievements. "AuDHD women from underrepresented backgrounds finally understood themselves. Professionals gained a new framework. It was novel, innovative and a bid to stop the medical gaslighting." But the thing she is most proud of, the thing closest to her heart, is The Neurodivergent Phoenix. "Phoenix means rising from the ashes. We zigzag through life, but when you step into your truth, you rise stronger, more discerning, unapologetic."

She also credits spirituality for helping her step into visibility. "It wasn't until I consulted an astrologer that I thought, ok, there is a reason for all this. He told me my life purpose is in my career. Human design told me I'm a Manifestor, which meant I couldn't hide. And it hit my deepest fear. Being seen makes you vulnerable, but I embraced it."

Out of this came her AuDHD Intersectional Scientific Framework: Tip of the Iceberg (TOTI Framework). "It has layers, role overload, daily challenges, trauma history, relationships, support network, hormones, co-occurring conditions, down to your innate neurobiological wiring to help professionals see the invisible layers that influence how we show up as AuDHD women. Most of the time, women hear, 'this woman is crazy,' and are assessed for BPD or EUPD. But many could be diagnosed with ADHD or autism if people knew where to look and provide adequate support earlier." Her book 'Tip of the ADHD Iceberg' extends this philosophy, blending science and spirituality into a practical anchor for those navigating late diagnosis.

Asked what she would change about her AuDHD, she doesn't hesitate. "Knowing I need time to switch gears and getting prepared for a transition, earlier. If I was ready 15 minutes earlier, so much anxiety and the ensuing consequences from being late could be avoided. It affects my children, too. When we rush to catch a train, my children are running with me, so they get anxious too." Yet there are qualities she would never part with. "My flood of ideas, not all good, but I love them. And my sense of justice, the need to change something that isn't working. Early in my career, I was told I was rude and socially unaware when I tried to improve the systems at work. I learned to people-please around it, to suppress my truth, but now I listen to my intuition. I've never been wrong. And I now run my own social impact company creating the change I want to see in the world."

Her advice to others is simple: "Follow your interests. Talk to a coach. My first coach stopped me from chasing my tail. Without her, ADHD Girls might not exist." To her younger self, she would say: "You will get out one day. Life will be great, not because of a man, but because of you. There will be shitty times, but good news is ahead."

For Samantha, the Phoenix isn't just a symbol, it's her life in motion. "We go through the highs and lows, but once you step into your truth, you rise from the ashes stronger, more discerning, unapologetic."

It is that unapologetic rise, visible to her children, her community, and the women she works with, that defines her story. Not the zigzags or the setbacks, but the way she continues to rise, again and again, and show others that they can too.

Website:	adhdgirls.co.uk
LinkedIn:	@samanthahiew
Instagram:	@samanthahiewphd

Claire Quigley Ward

All Aboard ADHD Podcast Host | Certified ADHD Coach |
Founder of ADHD Winchester

When Claire Quigley Ward walked into her GP's office with her 6 year old son, she wasn't thinking about ADHD. She was thinking about failure. However much she tried, the routines, the strategies, the patience, nothing seemed to work. Her toddler daughter had also faced some serious health challenges since birth, and with her son 'bouncing off the walls', Claire felt exhausted and lost. "I thought I was failing as a parent," she remembered. "It never crossed my mind that it might be ADHD."

That appointment changed everything. They were referred to child psychiatry and soon after, her son was diagnosed with ADHD. It was the first time Claire had ever heard the word connected to her life, and what she didn't know was that, at 41, she would discover that she also had ADHD. His diagnosis was the key to unlocking her own.

Today, Claire is a certified ADHD Coach, and the host of the All Aboard ADHD podcast. She has built a community where experts, parents and special guests share insights, strategies, and stories. For her, the mission is deeply personal: "I never wanted anyone to feel as alone as I had. That's why I do this work."

Like many women of her generation, Claire's ADHD went unnoticed for decades. Outwardly, she was sociable, bubbly, and always chatting. But school reports painted a different picture: bursts of brilliance alongside complete disengagement. "You could really see it," she said. "Hyperfocus in some subjects, zero interest in others. Constantly chatting, struggling to focus."

Her husband laughed when I asked if that still rang true: "She'll become an expert on something, get the job done, then move on. That suited her when she worked in TV. But she would never suit the corporate world; there's too much bureaucracy, and it would be too slow for her pace."

Internally, Claire's hyperactivity was constant, though largely invisible to others. "My hyperactivity is quite a mental one. I have a brain that just cannot stop. That's amazing and also tiring in equal measure."

Although she looked confident, she admits she often felt small. "I had such a low sense of self-worth. Much of my worth got tied up in productivity and achievements." Her son, who also has ADHD, sees another side of her, though: "She's more understanding of me because I have ADHD as well. It's helpful."

With her own diagnosis coming in reverse, she explained how the realisation of a genetic link became clear. "My dad is also a carbon copy of my son, and my daughter has since been diagnosed too". Through her own assessment, her school reports were enough to demonstrate it had clearly been present in childhood. The traits there in black and white.

Her husband remembers the validation relief of her diagnosis: "I just wanted her to worry less about what anybody else thinks. Be comfortable in her own skin and know how brilliant she is without trying any harder." For Claire, the diagnosis was less of a lightning bolt, and more of a slow dawning. "Every day, even now, I discover something new about myself. Time blindness, waiting mode, working memory. It's like building a picture piece by piece."

Her career, like her ADHD, was never linear. As a former TV Producer, she thrived in television, events, and high-energy environments, but struggled in slower, more conventional roles. The work she is most proud of came almost by accident. "The podcast. Out of everything I've done, it's the thing I'm most proud of." There is a calm sense of pride as she describes hitting 'record' for the first time. "I thought, why not just record one episode? I figured maybe no one would listen, so what did I have to lose? And it snowballed from there."

Eighteen months later, the All Aboard ADHD podcast had grown entirely organically. Claire poured her coaching income into bringing it to life and driving it forward, but the reward was worth it. "The sense of achievement when I receive a message from someone I've never met, sharing how hard things have been for them, and saying my podcast helped, that's possibly the greatest feeling in the world."

Her husband could see exactly why the work she does now suits her: "Being her own boss is the perfect role. There's no-one holding the brakes. If she sees ten steps ahead, she just goes and does it. It's a superpower for accomplishing things."

Claire is quick to acknowledge the challenges. The exhaustion, her struggles with working memory, and that if it isn't written down, it's gone. "My brain never stops. Without my scaffolding, reminders, lists, diaries, everything would fall apart."

She admits that interruptions can provoke a sharp internal reaction. "I'm not a rageful person but because it takes so much effort to get into a flow state, and because I struggle with transitions, when I get pulled out of hyperfocus, the rage is real. Parenting with that is tough, because you know you'll get interrupted. Sometimes I avoid starting things altogether to avoid the frustration." Her son has noticed the same thing: "If you're trying to explain something to her that isn't related to the task she's doing, she doesn't really pay attention because she's focused on that thing."

Her husband reflects how much Claire needs to switch off, and rest. She struggles, she can't do it, even when it's really needed.

But alongside the challenges are clear strengths. "I've developed a really strong sense of intuition," Claire reflects. "I'm good at reading people and situations. Sometimes it can be a curse, but it's also a strength." Her son is more matter of fact: "If you need something, she's determined to do it as quickly as possible." Her husband agrees: "If she's determined, she'll go through walls to do what needs to be done and can map steps ahead. That's her biggest skill."

Deadlines and pressure environments also bring out the best in her. "Creative problem-solving, body doubling, accountability, they're important for me. If you want me at my best, give me a deadline. That's why TV worked so well, constantly moving forward, novelty, energy. It played right into my strengths."

Looking back, Claire recognises the cost of masking, and people-pleasing, acknowledging how she's struggled with prioritising herself or asking for help. She shares that she feels she's self-sacrificed a lot and tried to be someone who didn't put others out. This came with constant over-apologies, and not advocating for her own needs. She tries hard now, and with the recognition from her family that she struggles to switch off and rest, she is getting better at it, sometimes. Her husband adds another perspective: "She doesn't take compliments very well. She hears them, but it doesn't go deep enough because she's already on to the next thing. Little and often helps."

One of the hardest patterns for her to shake is the belief that she is never enough. "Even after diagnosis I sometimes think, am I ADHD enough? Because I can manage things. But if you took away my scaffolding, it would all fall apart."

Her husband sees it differently. To him, the issue isn't a lack of ability, but the fact she rarely gives herself credit. "She doesn't realise how brilliant she is, because she never rests on one thing before she's on to the next."

If she could change one thing about her ADHD, Claire wouldn't erase it. Her wish would be to have a volume control in her brain, the ability to turn parts of her ADHD down, so she can rest when she needs to, without feeling guilty.

To her younger self, her advice is heartfelt: "You are enough. Trust your intuition. Believe in yourself, and don't keep yourself small. What feels like a struggle now will become your strength later. And you don't have to do it all alone."

For others just starting their entrepreneurial journey, she offers encouragement rooted in experience. The advice to remember, you are not alone. The importance of finding people to support you, your tribe, reach out to them, and be authentic, and honest. "Trust in yourself, believe in yourself, trust your guts."

Her son's reminder is shorter: "You've got this". Her husband's words are just as grounded: "We're grateful for everything she does".

Claire's story shows her journey of discovery, resilience, and relentless motion. From the mother who once sat in a GP's waiting room, convinced she was failing as a parent, to the ADHD coach, and podcast host who now reaches thousands, she has transformed not just her own understanding but the lives of those around her.

Her husband calls her an 'organising maestro'. Her son describes her as 'entertaining', and 'understanding' because of their shared ADHD. Between them, they capture what Claire sometimes misses: the brilliance in her relentlessness, the empathy in her advocacy, and the community she has built so others don't feel alone.

For Claire, ADHD is both exhausting and extraordinary in equal measure. It is the scaffolding that keeps life moving; the intuition to read a room, the hyperfocus that fuels her work, and the restlessness that drives her forward. She may not always pause long enough to take in her achievements, but those around her do. In their words lies the truth she most needs: she's got this.

Website: www.allaboardadhd.com
LinkedIn: @claire-quigley-ward
Instagram: @allaboardadhd

Natasha Davies

Founder of ND Organisational Dynamics Ltd |
Head of Research & Policy at ADHD 360 |
Executive ADHD Coach | Author & Writer

"Until the age of 35, I thought I was too much: too fast, too intense, yet never quite enough. Then came the word: ADHD. Suddenly, the story of my life made sense. Not an excuse, but an explanation. A missing piece that helped me see my strengths more clearly."

Today, Natasha (Tasha) Davies, professionally Natasha Scott (her maiden name), is Head of Research and Policy at ADHD 360, and Founder of ND Organisational Dynamics. Back in 2005, she joined the NHS as a filing clerk, working her way up to Director over two decades. Over the last few years, she has worked in Mental Health with a focus on improving quality and experience for patients, particularly across crisis and neurodivergent services. But her story is not measured by titles; it is one of grit, determination, and a relentless tenacity to keep moving forward.

Tasha grew up in Gloucestershire, the eldest of two girls, in a household marked by both love and difficult times. Her dad worked away when she was younger, and her mum, 'strong and resilient', held everything together.

Growing up, she always felt like she wasn't good enough and that she had to prove herself, and she shares how that became her inner narrative. At school, this was no different. Whilst she was creative and determined, thriving in subjects she enjoyed, she was easily distracted in others, with teachers noticing both her spark and her struggle. Music was always her passion, and from age 5, she began teaching herself piano by ear, going on to achieve Grade 7 by GCSEs. In 6th Form, she found adapting to a new teacher's rigid style difficult as it was less about the music and more about academia. "He sucked the joy out of it for me. I regret to this day that I let my ability slip, because music had been such a big part of who I was."

From an early age, Tasha's independence shone through. At 12, she worked in the local pub setting up skittles, determined to buy a mobile phone that her parents doubted she would save for. The challenge spurred her on – and she did it. From age 15, weekend jobs became her norm: hairdressing, retail, beauty, and waitressing. At 16, she stepped into the NHS, taking on admin shifts in her mum's department. Evenings were spent studying Beauty and Holistics three nights a week and doing her A Levels in the day. A year into 6th Form, she left to focus fully on the course and go full-time in the admin roles at the hospital. "Whilst everyone else was out having fun, I was working. I didn't mind; I enjoyed what I was doing."

That admin role developed, and within two years, she was promoted to Senior Oncology Medical Secretary. "I had no degree, no formal qualifications, but I grafted and worked my way up. I cared deeply about the role and the difference I was making at a time that was the hardest for many of the patients we looked after." Looking back, her husband describes this as one of her defining traits: "Her ability to make things happen where others would quit."

Those early admin roles led to managing admin teams, then the challenge of running day-to-day operations across different services. From there, she shifted into system-level work, shaping pathways across health, and later a national role as a Quality Improvement advisor, helping to build a better culture, drive improvement, and create better experiences for patients and staff.

Despite her progress, Tasha carried a subtle worry that plagued her. "I always thought the reason I didn't feel good enough, or was overlooked, was because I didn't have a degree. Nobody ever said

160

that, but I believed it." In 2015, she was offered the opportunity to study for a Master's in Healthcare Leadership alongside her work. She accepted it, despite it coming at a time of turbulence and, later, her mum's cancer diagnosis. "It nearly broke me. But in a lot of ways, it rebuilt me too."

Yet through that time, her husband reminded her of what really defined her: "The things that drew me to Tasha were that our values were strongly matched. She is relentless and determined, even in the face of obstacles or barriers. She is driven by doing good and helping people. If she has something to achieve, she will go after it with absolute commitment. She is brilliant, kind, thoughtful, and empathetic."

Becoming a mum, something Tasha had always wanted but had been unsure if it would happen, came in late 2018. Overjoyed, they welcomed their son. However, motherhood collided with grief when her mum's cancer returned. "My husband had proposed in early 2018, but we put wedding plans on hold when I found out I was pregnant. When my Mum's cancer returned in early 2019, we both agreed to bring it forward and have a small family wedding while she was still well, before treatment began. Within two weeks, I'd planned the whole thing, with a baby in tow, and we were walking down the aisle. It was everything: connection, a genuine partner in life, and having the people we loved most there with us." Torn between the joy of new motherhood and the weight of anticipatory grief, Tasha poured her emotions into something creative whilst on maternity leave. What began as raw Instagram posts about the reality of motherhood became The Clumsy Explorer eMagazine, her first published digital product, something her Mum was at the very heart of. "I interviewed people like Gaby Roslin and Anna

Whitehouse. They didn't know me, but they trusted me and said yes. After she died and during the pandemic (and my second maternity leave!) the magazine became a tribute to my mum, my way of healing, and proof that even in the darkest times, I could still create something beautiful." Through this, she grew in confidence as a writer and editor, paving the way for collaborations that would later evolve into her coaching and consultancy business.

Her mum died, aged 53, when Tasha was 12 weeks pregnant with her daughter, just 3 weeks before the Covid lockdown. "Every inch of me wanted to crumble. But being pregnant, I couldn't. My husband was phenomenal. There's no way we would have made it through all of that without him. He was, and still is, our rock. It was hard, but I found ways to redirect my grief, to keep going for my kids, and to stay on a journey of making a difference."

Those years almost broke her, but they also rebuilt her. Her husband reflects on how those experiences shaped her resilience: "She's worked relentlessly hard to get to where she is, with an internal commitment to keep making a difference. It's rarely about herself; she gives so much to help others. Family bereavements, especially losing her mum so young, have not halted her determination, but have made her who she is. They have perhaps even pushed her determination further."

Over the next few years, grief and anxiety were always close by. Sharing her struggles with a close friend, who had recently been diagnosed with ADHD, made everything click. "After that, I remember telling my husband I thought I might have ADHD, and he agreed, sharing he'd always suspected he did too. At the time, rather than let me spiral, he reminded me of the positive things it meant: energy, creativity, determination, empathy." In March 2023, after years of sitting on a waiting list, she finally heard the words: You have ADHD. "I burst into tears. My experience was robotic and lacked empathy. I was never given any follow-up, treatment or support, but at last I had the missing piece of the puzzle."

She was later re-referred to ADHD360 who re-confirmed her diagnosis, this time, combined ADHD, and finally provided her with the support and understanding that had been missing from her original diagnosis. "The understanding and patience from my clinician has been incredible, I'm so grateful. Medication hasn't been a magic fix, but it's helping me see what's possible."

When asked about her ADHD strengths, Tasha names these as creativity, empathy, determination, and 'dog with a bone' persistence. She recalls in 2014, when she ran her first marathon. "I was told I couldn't do it. That was like a red rag to a bull. My mum said, 'If you put your mind to it, you can.' She was right."

But the challenges are just as real: crippling RSD, self-doubt, hyperfocus, and compulsion to 'get things done' no matter the personal cost. Time blindness is another constant battle. "In my teens and 20s, my family would tell me to be somewhere 30 minutes earlier, so I'd arrive on time. Now, I'm the one rushing everyone out of the house with five minutes to spare, having crammed in too many unrealistic tasks. 'Tasha Time', as my family call it, is chaotic, especially for the kids." She feels fortunate that her husband and many close friends also have ADHD, meaning she never has to mask around them – they simply get her. Finding that tribe took time, but it's something she's deeply grateful for.

Her husband recognises both her brilliance and her struggles: "When she's got something in her mind, that's all that exists. That's hard when it's a problem that isn't hers because she won't let go until it's solved. Sometimes there isn't a fix, and she can't always help. But when her energy is channelled positively, the results are extraordinary – outcomes others wouldn't even dream of. I know Tasha can achieve whatever she sets her mind to, and I'll always believe in her abilities."

Professionally, in 2024 being made redundant after 20 years in the NHS could have broken her, but instead, it became her pivot point. "It was half my life, my identity, tangled up with my mum, who'd helped me get my first job there. I questioned my purpose. But I took a leap. I had 20 years NHS experience, a Master's, my exec coach training and ADHD coach certification. With my husband's backing, I set up my business, providing consultancy and executive ADHD coaching, which I have built up since then."

That leap opened unexpected doors. Tasha messaged Dr Phil Anderton on LinkedIn around the work ADHD360 was doing. This led to collaboration on the economic impact of undiagnosed ADHD, a paper Phil commissioned Tasha to write that they later presented together at a webinar. "It was the first time I stepped into my own credibility as a business owner." Now part-time Head of Research and Policy at ADHD 360, she supports important work on ADHD in women, co-occurring conditions, the justice system, education and policy. Her role is new still, but she sees the opportunities there are to make a difference in how neurodivergent people are supported. Soon after joining ADHD 360, Phil asked her to co-author a book sharing real-life stories of ADHD, grit and success, something that has been hugely fulfilling. "It's been a labour of love and I'm so proud of the work we have done. Co-authoring a book is something I never thought I would do and it's been an absolute privilege. I hope readers find strength in words of motivation, courage in shared stories, and comfort in knowing they belong to a tribe wired just like them. I know I have when doing the interviews."

If Tasha could change any of her ADHD, she shares. "I'd get rid of rejection sensitivity dysphoria (RSD); it's so draining. I'd also love to feel more balanced. When I'm up, I'm bouncing off the walls. When I'm down, it's exhausting. I crave more calm for my kids, my husband, and me." Her advice to other entrepreneurs with ADHD is simple: "Be careful what you read. Cut out the noise. Don't let memes trivialise your struggles. Find your tribe and believe in yourself, you already know what you're capable of."

To her younger self, she'd share the mantra her mum often quoted from The Wizard of Oz: "You've always had the power, my dear, you just had to believe it." Her husband's words, which he would want her always to remember, are both a love letter and a truth she is still learning to hold: "You are brilliant, capable of so much, and stronger than you know. Don't let anxiety or not feeling good enough get in the way. Breathe, slow down, you are enough."

Tasha is still learning to believe that. But her story of courage, resolve, motherhood, grief, and reinvention proves it has been true all along.

Website: www.nd-od.com
               www.natashascottcoaching.com
LinkedIn: @natashadavies-id
Instagram: @weareNDOD | @thisistashadavies

CHAPTER 3

The Creatives, Makers & Storytellers*

*This is where imagination meets action. These are the artists, makers, writers, and storytellers who use their craft to shift perspectives, spark emotion and bring ideas to life. Through their creativity, they challenge stereotypes, inspire change, and remind us of the power of self-expression.

Ella Fielding

Artist | Sculptor | TV Personality

When Ella Fielding first picked up a chainsaw, she wasn't following a plan. She was following a feeling. It was a spark of excitement that lit her up from the inside out. What she didn't know then was that she was carving out more than sculptures. She was carving out a life that made sense to her brain.

"I didn't sit down and think, 'I want to be a chainsaw carver,'" she explains. "I just followed what excited me."

Based in the south of England, Ella is now a full-time sculptor and artist known for her striking, large-scale wood carvings. Her pieces are raw, expressive, and full of character. But the real power behind her work lies in the story she brings with it. Her story is one of rediscovery, of building a business and an identity that embraces her neurodivergent brain.

Before she found carving, Ella's early years were marked by confusion, frustration and feeling constantly out of sync. She had glue ear as a child, which impacted her hearing and later she was diagnosed with dyslexia. But ADHD was never mentioned.

She recalls that as a young child, maybe 3 or 4 years old, "I'd be playing up and my mum would send me into another room and I'd sit there hyper-focused, hitting the wall repeatedly. That didn't bother me, but it drove everyone else mad."

Secondary school was particularly tough. She was labelled disruptive, emotional, and intense. Nothing seemed to fit. However, Ella describes how lucky she was to have parents who were tolerant, supportive, and most importantly, advocated for her. They recognised that she needed something different and her mum, a teacher, advocated fiercely for her, eventually helping Ella leave school at 14 and move into college early. It was there, in a more adult and self-directed environment, that everything changed.

"I could be myself. Wear what I wanted. Pick what I wanted to study. And suddenly, I loved learning. I became obsessed with it."

That sense of agency stayed with her. When she went on to study sculpture at university, she opted to shadow practising artists rather than write a dissertation and says, "It was a no-brainer for me. Write a dissertation or get stuck in and create with some incredible artists whilst keeping a diary about it." She remembered seeing a sculpture at Glastonbury years earlier that had stopped her in her tracks - something about it had resonated with her deeply.

When thinking about who to shadow, this artist immediately sprang to mind and she was determined to track him down, which she did. To her delight, he agreed to let her shadow him and that's where she first picked up a chainsaw. He handed it to her and said, "Have a go."

"The adrenaline and directness clicked with my brain instantly," she says. "I learn through my hands. If I've done something physically, I remember it. Words, lectures - they just don't stick."

The second artist she shadowed worked in a very different way: calm, precise, methodical. While that style didn't ignite her in the same way, Ella appreciated the contrast. It helped her understand that there's no one 'right' way to create, and that creativity can take many forms.

But even as she carved out her creative path, life remained exhausting. Diagnosed with ADHD at 37, Ella spent most of her life not knowing why she felt so out of step with the world. The demands of conventional life left her burnt out, paralysed, and overwhelmed.

"It was like holding a huge pile of laundry with socks falling out the sides," she says. "I wasn't lazy. I was paralysed. I felt like everyone outside was thinking I was lazy and that made me spiral."

Her ADHD diagnosis came after a particularly intense period of parenting and running her business. She reached out for dyslexia support through Access to Work, something she'd accessed back in college, and was paired with a brilliant coach.

"She kept saying, 'With your ADHD...' and I kept correcting her, saying, 'Oh, this is embarrassing, I don't have ADHD, I have Dyslexia'. But after a few sessions, she just said, 'Ella, you definitely have ADHD'."

That moment of recognition changed everything. Her husband, Phil, remembers the day well. "She called me and said, 'I think this explains everything,' and I just said, 'Yeah, of course it does'." It was this that then prompted her to get a referral.

Phil recalls researching neurodivergence and that this "really helped me understand how to support her better. Not saying things like 'Why haven't you done this?' because that just doesn't help anyone."

Parenting in those early years wasn't easy. Ella was pouring all her energy into being a present mum and running and growing a creative business, without knowing she was operating at full capacity all the time. "She'd pour herself into work, then come home and crash. There was never a middle ground," says Phil.

Ella adds, "The other mums would always be on time for the baby classes, and I'd be running in late, totally disorganised and feeling ashamed. I don't know how they did it!" She reflects on that time as a blur of survival. "I was trying to be everything to everyone. And I was barely holding it together."

The diagnosis brought her clarity and self-compassion. It gave her a new lens through which to view her past, her work, and her needs. She began to manage her energy differently, building in recovery time and questioning what she really wanted to say yes to. "I used to think I was anti-social or rude. But now I know I just didn't have a buffer."

Phil noticed the shift too. "She started giving herself permission to rest. She began saying no to things. That was the biggest change."

Ella's work, she now sees, is perfectly ADHD-friendly. Her days are full of movement, creativity, autonomy, and fast-paced decision-making. "Every day, I remind myself: I choose to do this. I get to do this."

Phil agrees. "Professionally, her ADHD is probably what makes her incredible at what she does. I honestly don't think she could work in a conventional job, she just wouldn't thrive. Her creativity, spontaneity, and ability to hyperfocus are her superpowers."

She says that when she gets into hyperfocus, the world fades away. She can stay up until 3am finishing a piece or researching something she's curious about. And when inspiration strikes, there's no waiting. "There's a lot of impulsive hyperfocus too. We'll have a brief conversation about something for the house, and before I've even finished my sentence, it's been ordered on Amazon," says Phil with a smile.

When thinking about the things that are challenging living with an ADHD Entrepreneur, Phil says that the pace and unpredictability can be challenging, but he wouldn't trade it. "I never know quite what's coming next, but I kind of enjoy that unpredictability now. If you'd asked me in the early days, I'd have said something like 'Her shoes are everywhere!' But now we've been together so long, I've adapted to her way of being.

The biggest challenge is probably trying to run a household when you've got two chaotic people. Things fall through the cracks sometimes. But we muddle through. It's carnage, but no one dies. The kids are happy. We're happy. That's what matters."

He describes watching her grow into her creative identity as one of the most rewarding parts of their life together. "When I met her, she was doing casual events work and wasn't loving it. Then she started to take carving seriously. I tried to support her however I could. And now, she's phenomenal at it. I'm honestly in awe of what she can do."

Ella doesn't always see it. "She's not someone who wants constant praise or validation, but she does need reassurance sometimes," says Phil. "She doubts herself more than she should. When she gets good feedback from clients, it really means a lot. It gives her the fuel to keep going."

When asked to describe her in a few words, he doesn't hesitate. "Loving. Funny. One of a kind. There's honestly nobody else like her."

And when asked the one ADHD trait he wouldn't change for the world? "Her energy. Her spontaneity. The way she just goes for things. That's what makes her who she is. I wouldn't change it."

That spontaneity has led to some wild adventures. "Her work is exciting; she's always off doing something mad like filming for Discovery or creating giant sculptures."

Their life together is built on shared values. "We've always prioritised adventure and experiences, not material stuff. We're not about 'the next car' or another house renovation. It's more like, 'Where's the next adventure? What's the next big idea?' And I love that about our life."

Ella, too, sees her neurodivergence as a core part of who she is. "People say, 'You don't seem ADHD.' But they're looking for a stereotype. My ADHD shows up in joy, in energy, in parenting. It gives me permission to be unapologetically me."

To others who are still figuring it out, she says: "Be kind to yourself. Follow what lights you up. Not every idea has to work. You only need one to change everything."

And to those who love someone with ADHD? Phil says it best: "Give them space to be themselves. Help them rest. Don't try to make them fit. Celebrate their spark."

Website: EllaFielding.com
LinkedIn: @ella-fielding-sculptor
Instagram: @ella.fielding.sculptor

Polly Hazlewood

Co-Host of Dirty Mother Pukka Podcast | Somatic Sexologist

When Polly Hazlewood introduces herself, she does it with both humour and honesty. She's the co-host of Dirty Mother Pucker, the podcast she runs with her best friend, and a qualified somatic sexologist working with couples, and individuals.

Her brands Polly Amorous and Happily Unfckd aren't just playful titles; they embody her mission to help people unfck themselves from social and cultural conditioning, remove shame, and to live the lives they truly want. "I want people to feel free," Polly says. "Free of shame, free of judgement, free to live the lives they actually desire." It's bold, disruptive, and deeply personal, like Polly herself.

From a young age, she was different. At school, she was always inventing, writing plays, and making her siblings perform musicals in the living room. She was sociable and playful, yet on the inside, she struggled with concentration, drifting away until teachers caught her daydreaming.

She learned to mask early, a chameleon who became whoever she thought people wanted her to be. She wasn't popular, never 'cool' but she was creative, and full of ideas. Humour was her way in, her way of staying safe. Still, she carried a deep-rooted belief that something was wrong with her.

At university, she thrived for the first time, but afterwards drifted again, trying different jobs, even founding a theatre company with a friend that she enjoyed running for a while.

Later, it seemed teaching could be a sensible path for her, but in honesty, whilst her passion was there, the expectation of teaching in the English education system was a far cry from what she thought it should be. Seeing creativity, and playfulness be squeezed out of children by a system still rooted in Industrial Revolution standards was unbearable. "It was like watching light go out of their eyes," she says. "They came in buzzing with curiosity and within a year, it was gone."

Then came a major turning point: the chance to design a brand-new private school from scratch. The building was an old library, empty when she arrived. She poured herself into it, every evening, weekend, and through the school holidays. She was shaping the curriculum, culture, and community from the ground up. "We had no books, no furniture, nothing," she remembers. "But it was ours to build. It mattered. It felt purposeful."

For months, she split her time between teaching in another school by day and working on the new school by night. She'd arrive at 6pm and stay until past midnight, piecing together systems, policies, and learning spaces. Summers were spent on site, covered in dust and paint, because she believed so fiercely that education should nurture rather than diminish. Exhausting, yes, but for the first time she felt she was doing work that truly mattered.

Life shifted again when her then-husband took a job in Los Angeles, and together they moved to the other side of the world. Overnight, she went from having a purpose and identity to being labelled a 'trailing spouse' with no right to work, and little sense of who she was. That loss ran deep, but nothing could prepare her for what came next.

Pregnant with twins, she hoped for joy and a new chapter, only to find herself in a world she could never have imagined. Her long-awaited babies were born with a genetic condition so rare it had never been recorded before. They spent 56 days in intensive care, and every day was filled with uncertainty. "You expect some joy as a new mum," Polly says softly, "But there was none. Just machines, hospital corridors and so much fear." The future felt fragile, the twins prognosis bleak. Instead of the excitement she had longed for, she was left clinging to each moment, just trying to hold it all together.

The day-to-day reality was relentless. Polly became their nurse, physio, OT, and carer, administering medications through the night, attending multiple hospital appointments each week, learning medical terminology on the fly. Her husband worked away. She went into survival mode, laser-focused on the here and now, never looking too far ahead, just putting one foot in front of the other. "I didn't Google anything, I still haven't if I'm honest," she says. "I didn't want to know. The only way I could cope was to be in the here and now."

She didn't feel the joy she thought she was meant to. Instead, she felt like a failure. "My body couldn't even produce healthy children," she recalls. That period changed everything. Eventually, the weight of it would tear their marriage apart.

After three years, they came back to the UK. Polly was a full-time mum, but she was lost. Her best friend suggested reviving a podcast she'd previously hosted, but this time, with Polly by her side, to be her co-host.

Normally, she would have talked herself out of it, convinced she had nothing to offer, and not dared to do anything outside of her comfort zone. But after everything she'd been through, she said yes. That yes became a lifeline, and a way to reclaim parts of her she thought she'd lost. "It was laughter, it was tears, it was extraordinary women telling extraordinary stories. It gave me back a piece of myself."

That courage led to another pivotal decision: retraining as a sexologist. On her 42nd birthday, she put herself first for the first time. She left her marriage, began to explore her sexuality for the first time, and followed the calling she had always felt but never allowed herself to pursue. "I've always been a sexual being, but I was restricted. This was me finally stepping into who I really am."

It was also a period of rediscovery, of friendships, of freedom, and of play. Since then, she has fallen in love again, and found a connection built on laughter, honesty, and ease. "I've never laughed so much in my life," she says. "It feels fun. It feels like home." She's unapologetic about the exploits that mark her new chapter: from travelling to see clients with her 'find yourself' kit, and having a vibrator accidentally switch on in her bag on the train ("I quickly exclaimed, as everyone around me could hear it, 'Oh, my toothbrush again, it's right at the bottom of my bag!'"), to hosting a live *Dirty Mother Pucker* show in the West End with her heavily pregnant co-host.

Through it all, there has been laughter, joy, and so much fun. This is Polly: exploration without shame, joy without judgment, and a life now unbounded by the expectations of others.

This also led to another revelation. For years, Polly had felt chaotic, forgetful, and lost in constant overwhelm. She genuinely believed she might have early dementia. A friend described her own ADHD experience, and for Polly, it was like hearing her own life described with absolute clarity. Two years later, she received her own diagnosis. At first, she doubted it, convinced herself she'd somehow tricked the doctors. But then everything clicked. Reading about girls with ADHD brought her to tears. The grief of a lifetime of feeling like a failure poured out — and alongside it came relief and self-compassion. "It was like somebody turned the lights on in a dark room I'd been wandering my whole life," she says.

Now, Polly sees her ADHD as woven through her story. The creativity, empathy, pattern-spotting, risk-taking, and resilience that defined her life were all there in plain sight. So too were the struggles with detail, admin, transitions, and the day-to-day grind.

But she no longer sees them as proof she's broken. She is learning to reframe them as part of her whole story. "For years, I thought being disruptive was a weakness," she says. "Now it's my strength. It's my brand."

Looking back, she says to her younger self: "You're not the problem. The system is. Your playful, bonkers, big-idea nature is your superpower. Don't ever change."

Today, Polly is designing a life that feels like hers. She channels her energy into her coaching, her brands, her podcast, and the movement she's building. Whether it's helping a woman rediscover pleasure after motherhood, sparking debates about shame, or simply making people feel seen, and valued, Polly is disruptive, visionary and human to her core. "I've designed a life I actually want to lead," she says. "Playful, joyful, purposeful." And this time, it isn't about surviving or fitting into someone else's mould, it's about living on her own terms, laughing loudly, loving deeply, and proving that being 'too much' was always more than enough.

Website:	www.polly-amorous.com
	www.happilyunfckd.com
Instagram:	@dirtymotherpukka | @happilyunfckd | @polldoll
Podcast:	Dirty Mother Pukka (Found on all platforms)

Alan P Brown

Founder of ADD Crusher™ | Author | Speaker |
ADHD & Productivity Coach

It was halfway through senior year, and the guidance counsellor pulled him aside, looked him straight in the eye, and said, "Alan, you're not graduating".

For Alan P Brown, now Founder of ADD Crusher™, Author, Speaker, and a certified ADHD and productivity coach, the words landed with a mix of disbelief, and inevitability. Back then, he was coasting along on his humour and last-minute scrambles, skipping classes for weeks at a time and hanging out with what he calls 'a bit of a rough crowd'. Schoolwork rarely got done, and even when it did, it felt like he was running on empty.

"I always felt different," Alan recalls of his childhood. "From as far back as 4 or 5, I was the clown, the class clown. I struggled to read, and by the time I was 13 or 14, I'd only ever finished one book, and a thin paperback one at that."

His need for belonging and dopamine made risky behaviour magnetic. By 12, he was smoking, drinking, and skipping school for weeks. Somehow, he scraped through. Later on, at university, it would take him 10 years to complete a 4-year degree. Along the way, life was a string of bartending jobs, a stint as what he jokes was 'a not very successful drug dealer', and the occasional hustle that kept him afloat but never fulfilled.

"I realised I was self-medicating. When I was taking drugs, I was actually getting good grades, because that was the stimulant. Cocaine seemed to fire up a brain that otherwise felt foggy and slow."

Reaching his 30's, Alan finally got what he calls 'a real job' in advertising. But the same struggles remained: long hours, plenty of effort, and yet little to show in terms of progress. He was floundering along in a role for years that was associated with those in their 20's. Then came a twist of fate. In a meeting with his boss, he shared with Alan that his son had just been diagnosed with ADHD and that he, realising the similarities in himself through his son's assessment and diagnosis, had also been diagnosed.

For Alan, this was a lightbulb moment. "As he described the traits of him and his son to me, I realised, "Oh my God, that's me.'"

Alan booked an appointment with his doctor, a well-established practice on the Upper East Side of Manhattan, only to be dismissed. "He told me ADHD was a myth created by the media and I just needed to do more crossword puzzles. That's a direct quote from the doctor." Alan went back to meandering through his role in advertising and it would take five years before that initial seed of realisation would begin to grow again.

Fast forward those five years, recently divorced, and living in the East Village, NYC, he noticed a flyer in The Village Voice for an Adult ADHD Support Group titled 'ADHD: The Doctors who get it and the doctors who don't'. "That lit me up," he says. He went along, listened, it reignited that initial realisation for Alan and set him off on a path to, this time, find out the truth about his brain. Soon afterwards, he found a psychiatrist and booked in for an ADHD assessment. The psychiatrist recognised his symptoms within a minute. "You are a classic case," the doctor said.

Medication was prescribed cautiously, given Alan's history with alcohol and drugs, but eventually the right combination clicked and Alan shares that today, he's still on the same medications, albeit his dosage has steadily decreased over the years. "It felt like my brain just turned on. Suddenly, I could read a report, write clearly, and think clearly. It was liberating."

The results were startling. "I went from being a 37-year-old account executive earning an OK salary (although usual for 22 year olds) to a six-figure salary, Vice President, Management Director, and Employee of the Year, at the biggest ad agency in the country. All within two and a half years. That was the power of diagnosis."

Recognition and stability didn't hold him for long and just four years after diagnosis, only months after being named Employee of the Year, his need for dopamine and risk would take hold. An opportunity to co-found a startup with two brilliant partners presented itself and Alan couldn't turn it down. He quit advertising and moved into the world of startups, and entrepreneurs. "We had no money, no product, no investors, nothing but belief. Every day was a dopamine parade. It was exciting and terrifying at the same time."

That company, GoalQuest, was eventually sold for eight figures. Alan had already moved on, but the experience confirmed what he now calls one of his ADHD superpowers: risk-taking.

After leaving GoalQuest, he briefly returned to advertising, enjoying his most lucrative years. His diagnosis, coupled with the dopamine-fuelled rollercoaster of the GoalQuest years, had sparked a deeper curiosity about ADHD, and in particular, how his own brain was wired. He began designing hacks and strategies to keep his mind in check, and this became the catalyst for what came next.

In 2010, he took another leap. Born out of frustration, he began building ADD Crusher™, a platform of interactive videos and audios teaching ten core strategies for adults with ADHD. "I bought all these books about ADHD, and when I got home, I remembered, oh yeah, I'm a terrible reader. That became my inspiration. I wanted to make something ADHD-friendly, fun, visual, engaging." He channelled everything he had learned into what is today known as 'The #1 Program for ADHD Adults'.

He launched ADD Crusher™ in 2012, and around the same time, the President of the ADHD Coach Academy in the US persuaded him to become a certified coach. Today, Alan works as both a coach and an entrepreneur, with ADD Crusher™ still supporting people globally. "If you're going to put my name on something, I'd want it to be that I reached thousands and thousands of people with ADHD-friendly solutions that help them live to their potential."

Alan speaks readily about the strengths ADHD has given him. "Risk-taking is right up there, along with creativity. Entrepreneurship is a creative pursuit, and I think my more synaptic brain, not linear, but associative, helps me come up with ideas, navigate problems, and write." His restless curiosity, or what he calls his 'motor mind', fuels endless ideas and energy.

But that motor also exhausts him. "I am exhausted by my motor. The constant thinking, analysing, worrying, it drives anxiety. I've only recently, at 65, come to terms with how much anxiety I've carried all my life."

One of the most unusual aspects he shares openly is his obsessive-compulsive personality disorder (OCPD). "I think it's my defence against chaos. I have to maintain order, so I don't waste my precious mental energy." For Alan, that means rules. Everything has to be in its place, visual clutter eliminated. "I'll walk two flights of stairs just to put a dirty dish in the dishwasher. That sight of chaos taxes my brain."

His quirks even extend to hygiene. "Ok, this one is weird: I don't wash my hands immediately after using the bathroom. Instead, I walk to the kitchen and wash my hands there, and whatever's in the sink. Same amount of time, but I've done the dishes as well. It saves me time, reduces clutter, and I never have a sink full of dishes that I dread doing."

These rules, he admits, can cause friction at home. "Friends might say I'd be easier to travel with if I were less anxious. My wife sometimes gets frustrated with my little rules. But it's all about controlling chaos so I can protect my mental energy."

His wife, Rachel, describes living with Alan as "a wild ride of fear, excitement, boredom, anxiety, immense gratitude and laughter every single day." She calls it a daily exercise in patience and personal development, where the two of them lift each other up when it's been too long since there was a win, and where life is 'fun and interesting as hell'.

Those closest to him describe him as 'energetic, quirky, passionate' but also 'a little neurotic, impatient, and sometimes too much in the spotlight'. Rachel adds that Alan is a Renaissance man, "the quintessential enthusiast with a sidecar overflowing with justice and fairness." His compassion, she says, is "genuine and legendary," and he will get just as big and loud to celebrate someone as he will to defend them from injustice.

When it comes to guiding ADHD entrepreneurs, newly diagnosed or new to the world of entrepreneurship, he speaks from the heart but also from hard-won experience. "The first thing is make sure you have 'brain scaffolding'. My brain is such a floppy mess that I have to prop it up with tools, rules, hacks, and accountability. In the corporate world, your scaffolding is your boss and deadlines – adult supervision. As an entrepreneur, you need to build that for yourself, planners, alarms, rituals. However it works for you! Apps, paper, whatever. That's what will keep your brain from flopping out of your head and rolling around on the floor."

His own non-negotiables reflect this. A planner he checks daily, a nine-step morning ritual that takes four minutes but sets the tone, alarms for every important commitment, and when it's needed, reminders to do a mind-check in. "Those are the things that stop me from screwing up."

The second piece of advice he insists on is to forget time management. "It's all about energy management. You can have all the planners and apps in the world, but if you don't have energy, they're useless." For Alan, that means diet, exercise and sleep, his 'holy trinity'.
Rachel views this discipline differently: not just as structure, but as his way of protecting the limited window of optimal focus he has each day. She says Alan guards that time fiercely, cutting out distractions so he can bring his full self to the work that matters.

"If you can't rate yourself at least a 7 out of 10 on each of those, you're pushing a boulder up the hill. Exercise today gives you more energy tomorrow. Sleep deficit makes your ADHD worse. And knowing your strongest mental time of day is crucial. Mine is 7am to 11am. I guard that time, don't take meetings, and only do my hardest work then." It's advice born not just of study but of survival.

If he could speak to his teenage self, the boy barely scraping through high school, Alan knows exactly what he would say: "You feel different because your brain is different. That's OK. Be proud of it. It will make your life more interesting and fulfilling. Go ahead and be different." Rachel would want to remind him that he has always protected his uniqueness, that he grew up among tough guys but never lost his softness, curiosity, or vulnerability. She calls his masculinity 'protective, inclusive, and secure', something rare and precious, and a quality that creates safety for those around him.

What lingers after his story isn't the struggle, but his spark, the restless motor that once pulled him into chaos, and now powers change for thousands. Alan has shown that ADHD isn't a deficit to erase but a force to harness. From the class clown who almost didn't graduate, to the entrepreneur who built tools countless people now rely on, his life is proof that what once felt like chaos has become the foundation for change.

"I never thought I'd be able to do this, but I've reached thousands with ADHD-friendly solutions that help people live to their potential. That's no boast, it's just what I've been called to do." For Rachel, "It's peaks and valleys, but always progress, growth, and a lot of laughs along the way. The spark, the flirting with life, the social risk-taking, the verve that is Alan Brown. The world needs more Alan."

Alan doesn't claim perfection, only impact. And perhaps that's what makes his story resonate most: not that he mastered ADHD (he doesn't claim he has) but that he continues to learn, grow, and share, turning that journey into a legacy of clarity, courage, and change.

Website: addcrusher.com
LinkedIn: @alanpbrown
Instagram: @alanpbrown

Toby Goodale

Pilot | ex-Agricultural Specialist |
Tech Setup & Fixer at ADHD 360

When you first meet Toby Goodale, he has the easy confidence of someone who's learned to survive by throwing himself into whatever life offers. At 29, he's worked on building sites, driven 60-tonne potato harvesters, survived school exclusions, and carved his way into farming with no family ties to the land. But above all else, Toby is a pilot, a dream he clung to through years of false starts, setbacks, and disbelief from those around him.

"Getting my pilot's licence is my biggest achievement," Toby says. "Not because I wanted to prove it to anyone else, but because I wanted to prove it to myself. And maybe, yeah, to prove to my dad I could do it." Yet even as he says it, there's a flicker of doubt, a comment that it took him a long time, and as though he still isn't sure the achievement is as big as it sounds to anyone else.

School was never going to be easy. Toby was diagnosed with ADHD at 11, but back in 2007, a label was just that, a label. It didn't mean support.

"I wasn't an easy student. I went to seven different schools. I couldn't sit still, couldn't concentrate, and I just wanted to make people laugh. I was the class clown. My parents were constantly getting phone calls, and I was always on the edge of being excluded."

He remembers the diagnosis vividly, a long office in an old hospital, a stern-looking doctor, and his parents divided on the next steps. His dad wanted him to take medication, his mum didn't. In the end, nothing changed, and he didn't take medication. "Teachers knew, but there was no real support or understanding. I just lived with it."

For Toby, laughter was both a shield and a means of survival. "The best feeling was making the whole class laugh. That gave me pride, validation. It wasn't from a bad place; I just craved that spark."

Leaving school at 18, Toby found comfort in physical work. "On a building site, there are no books, just graft. I could focus on that." With money in his pocket for the first time, he booked flying lessons, a childhood dream sparked by drawing planes in the back of maths books (another thing he was always in trouble for at school).

But life wasn't smooth. He bounced between jobs: site labourer, digger driver, caretaker. Eventually he found his way into farming, despite having no experience, and none of the usual family ties to the industry. "Farming felt like an easy way for me to earn money, sitting in a tractor all day, getting paid to look out the window. But it was also boring, and the hours were relentless. You never knew when you'd finish or if you'd have a weekend."

Despite setbacks, being sacked after confrontations, quitting impulsively, and drifting into cocooned isolation, Toby pushed forward. His ADHD made routine unbearable yet also gave him bursts of drive to jump into the unknown. Farming was never planned, but that became an achievement in itself.

"Most people in farming inherit it. I started with zero experience, moving trays in a yard, and because of how hard I worked, I ended up driving the main potato harvester. That was a big deal for me. I learned by asking questions. If you don't know, ask. That's how I progressed." He shrugs as he says it, downplaying the reality; that carving out space in a generational industry, with no background at all, was extraordinary.

Flying, however, was always the golden thread. "It was my dream. But harvests, and long hours always got in the way. I'd get close to finishing, then have to stop for six weeks, sometimes because of work on the farm, sometimes because I just couldn't push myself to take that final step. Exams terrified me, so I kept putting them off."

Everything shifted when he joined Lincoln Aero Club. His instructor, David Jones, gave him belief. And then he met Phil Anderton.

"I didn't know who Phil was at first, just that I noticed he had a presence. I met him in the Clubhouse, and we got talking. He had also recently started flying lessons." Toby shares how, despite the success, experience, and seniority Phil clearly had, there was no arrogance to him, he was normal, welcoming, and just a kind, good man. "We started a study group with another pilot, Marcus Hudson, and called ourselves the 'Three Amigos'. We'd meet in pubs or go out for dinner. We'd revise together, push each other on. I needed that. Phil basically forced me to sit down and do the exams. Without that structure, I wouldn't have got there."

Eventually, Toby passed every exam, with only one fail along the way. Eight months ago, he earned his licence. "The day I called my dad to tell him I'd passed, he cried. It was the first time he'd ever said he was proud of me. That moment was worth everything." Toby retells it almost in disbelief, as if part of him still can't quite accept he deserves the pride it brought out in others.

The turning point came when Phil offered Toby a job at ADHD 360. "Farming was draining. I never had weekends off, I never knew what time I'd finish my work, as it could be extremely dependent on the weather. It was wearing me down mentally. Phil made me feel calm, like I could take the leap. I handed in my notice, even though it was tough after my old boss passed away, but it was the right move. For once, I put myself first."

For someone with ADHD, balance is often elusive. Structure helps. Knowing when a shift ends helps. At ADHD 360, Toby found that, and in turn, it has given him space for his flying, and space to think about his future, and opportunities. He also found his tribe, surrounded by other neurodivergent colleagues or people who get what it is to have ADHD.

Where ADHD weighs most heavily for Toby isn't in the cockpit or at work, it's at home. For years in farming, his days were swallowed by unpredictable hours, and relentless demands. He rarely had weekends off, and the sheer intensity left little space to think about anything else. Now, with a job that gives him structure, and free time, he's had to confront a different challenge: what happens when the pressure lifts and the executive-function wall appear.

"I don't see my family as much as I should. My grandparents are getting older, and I feel guilty about not visiting more. It's not that I don't care, I love them a lot, but I know I'm missing precious time with them" His niece has just turned two, and he shares he's only seen her a handful of times. "I'm missing out on her growing up, and that hurts. It's not that I don't want to be there, I do. Afterwards, I feel awful because I know what I've missed."

For Toby, this isn't about a lack of love or effort. It's the ADHD paralysis: that invisible wall that shows up in free time. Even simple things like getting in the car and making the journey can feel overwhelming. Hours slip by. Plans stay in his head, and he's left carrying the guilt of time lost. "That's something I'd change if I could."

He calls his mum often but laughs about how quick they can be. "They can last 15 seconds or five minutes. I can't sit on the phone for three hours, but she knows that's just me."

Beneath the jokes, and self-criticism is a simple truth: his family means the world to him. His absence is never about indifference; it's the ADHD paralysis that steals time. What he hopes they know is that the love has always been there, even when his actions don't show it in the way he wishes they could.

Ask Toby about the strengths of ADHD, and he doesn't hesitate. "Hyperfocus. If I love something, nothing can stop me. Flying is like that."

But the challenges weigh heavily too. "Lack of focus when I'm not interested. Terrible memory. Impulsiveness, especially with money. Anxiety that knocks me flat. ADHD is exhausting. Some days, I could sleep for nine hours and still be tired. But I wouldn't change much, life would be boring without it."

His friends wouldn't change him either. "If I walked into the pub as a normal, quiet person, they'd wonder what was wrong. ADHD makes me who I am."

Looking back to his younger self, aged 11, being diagnosed in that intimidating hospital office, Toby is reflective. "I'd tell myself to at least try a bit harder, listen more. But honestly, I wouldn't change much. I said I wanted to drive tractors, and fly planes, and I've done both. Not many people can say that."

And his advice to others? "Leap into the unknown. Be brave. Quitting farming for ADHD 360 was the first time I did it, and it worked out. Why shouldn't it for someone else?"

Toby knows ADHD hasn't made life easier: "ADHD is tiring, yeah. But it's fun. And I wouldn't swap it." However, it has given him the determination to push through and the curiosity to keep moving. It has shaped who he is: someone who doubts himself more than others see, but who has achieved more than he gives himself credit for. Someone who laughs loudest when others are laughing with him, who takes risks when life feels too small, and who has always, even if he didn't realise it, been reaching for the sky.

CHAPTER 4

The Leaders in Health & Social Impact*

*Here you will find people who are driving change in health, education, and the wider social landscape. They are advocates, reformers and change-makers who push for systems that work better for everyone. Their leadership is rooted in a clear sense of purpose and a commitment to making a difference.

Ryan Hopkins

Author & Speaker | Creating Healthier Workplaces
for Millions with JAAQ & Bupa

UNSTOPPABLE BY DESIGN

208

At 23 years old, Ryan Hopkins was standing on a mountainside in Ecuador, teaching himself Spanish, and helping an Indigenous family set up a hostel. He had left behind years of low self-worth, debt, and a body that had broken under pressure. For the first time in his life, he thought: 'I can do more than this. I am capable of doing more'.

Today, Ryan is Chief Impact Officer at JAAQ, Strategic Wellbeing Leader at Bupa and X Future of Wellbeing Leader at Deloitte. He has written a bestselling book, delivered TED Talks, and spoken to more than 110,000 people worldwide about wellbeing and the future of work. Yet the path that brought him here was anything but straight.

He was born almost half deaf, with what doctors described as 'floppy muscle tone'. He was late to walk, late to speak, late to do most things, though he remembers being "an old person in a kid's body. I used to speak like an adult when I was three. Probably disconcerting when you're chatting to a child and they're talking to you about the news."

School didn't come easily either. Undiagnosed ADHD and autism made him restless and distracted, and at 13, when his parents split, survival came first. His mum trained as a nurse whilst working every hour she could, with Ryan sometimes caring for his brothers. "I'd come home from school, cook dinner for them, and work in a barber shop a few nights a week. Study wasn't a priority."

By 16, he was working at Boots as a sexual health advisor, asking adults about their sex lives. "That builds confidence quickly," he laughs. But the confidence masked fragility. He thought his future was in the trades, following in his family's footsteps as a tradesman (an Electrician), until a rugby accident shattered his leg and with it, his apprenticeship. "My whole identity had been rugby, and being an electrician. Without that, who was I? I almost took my life and would have, if it hadn't been for my mum, and my Nan."

What followed was years of struggle. He battled bulimia for six years, carried shame in silence, and tried to outrun the feeling of being different. "I never saw another bloke speak about it. I thought I was a freak."

Travel became his escape and his new beginning. Backpacking through South America with a girlfriend, he obsessively taught himself Spanish, repeating words, scribbling them down each night, laughing when mistakes made him the butt of the joke. "I once asked, 'Where can one fuck a bus?' instead of 'catch a bus'. But I never forgot the word. That's how I learn: loud, public, self-deprecating." Within 6 months, he was fluent. Helping a family build a hostel on the side of a mountain helped him believe he was capable of more than his circumstances.

Going to University would offer another fresh start. He scraped by, getting into the only university that would take him. Later, he transferred to Oxford Brookes, and he thrived. Discovering he was dyslexic, and dyspraxic explained a lifetime of confusion. "I was 98th centile for verbal reasoning but about 15th for visual comprehension. Suddenly, it made sense why I needed to talk everything through." Still, the pressure he piled on himself was immense. "I was so anxious I couldn't leave my flat without feeling like I was going to piss myself. I came out in hives from the stress." Studying all day and working nights as a Bouncer. But, despite all that, he finished with a first-class degree.

Corporate life beckoned. After 150 graduate applications and 6 failed final interviews, Deloitte finally said yes. Digital transformation baffled him, but he gravitated to people, teams, and wellbeing. He began setting up small wellbeing initiatives long before it was mainstream. Not everyone welcomed his boundless energy. "At Deloitte, there's hierarchy. If you're a grad, you take notes. I wanted to do more. That rubbed people the wrong way."

The rejection hurt. He hadn't yet learned how to wear the professional mask, and pushback cut deeper when he tried to be himself. It wasn't until his return to Deloitte years later, leading teams and pioneering the Future of Wellbeing Consulting Business, that his ADHD diagnosis came. "My team said, 'We love working with you, but sometimes it's hard to follow where you're going'. I work at a million miles an hour. I'll jump around, I'll work evenings and weekends. I love it. But not everyone does."

When the diagnosis came, it was no surprise. "No shit, this makes sense," he says. By then, he had already built coping strategies. "But it gave me language to explain to others, and to myself." Autism followed a year later. His mum's reaction was simple: "We always knew you were different. But what good would it have done to change anything?"

As he puts it, Ryan's strengths and challenges are 'one and the same'. He doesn't relax well and feels like he might explode if he sits still. He fills the space with movement, training, cycling, walking, doing weights, listening to six or seven hours of podcasts daily on double speed, and reading a book weekly. It is how he wrote a bestselling book while working full-time. But the same intensity breaks him. He has torn muscles, collapsed under pressure, and once walked nineteen consecutive ultramarathons across Spain just to see what he was capable of. "I've hurt myself a lot to prove I'm worthy. I don't need to. But there are still elements of that in me."

Impatience is another thing that he struggles with. "If something needs doing, I'll do it now, no matter how much effort it takes. But I can't expect everyone else to work the way I do. That frustration is hard to manage."

Ryan worked for Sainsbury's during the pandemic. With the world in crisis, he found the space to prove what he could do. With no budget, but complete freedom, he was trusted to look after people in creative ways. "We were building stuff, and I saw the feedback in real time. That was when I thought: 'this is me'."

He started posting every day, experimenting with ideas in public. At first, it was cliché Instagram quotes. Then came 'toilet break wellbeing' - you flush and you flourish, recorded in short bathroom videos about the power of little changes and habits. "It looked like I had an OnlyFans channel with a ring light in my bathroom. But I loved it."

For 3 years, he posted without getting much back - 1 or 2 likes here and there, spending his weekends writing. "It must have been 675 hours of writing before anything came back. But I didn't care, I loved it."
Persistence paid off. His book launch brought tears, pride, and validation. His TED Talks reached global audiences. His speaking work now doubles what he once earned. More importantly, he shapes strategy with Bupa and formerly Deloitte, positively influencing the lives of over 1.3 million. And he's building something

bigger with JAAQ, the mental health platform he believes will change how the world talks about wellbeing.

The people around him see both sides. His girlfriend, also recently diagnosed, matches his honesty with her own. His mum has watched him torment himself to prove his worth and just wants him to be kinder to himself and his body. Colleagues can struggle with his relentless pace, but those who thrive under radical candour flourish beside him. "It's the hand that gives, and the hand that takes," Ryan says. "You have to shake hands with the devil. I wouldn't be who I am otherwise."

When asked what advice he would give to someone with ADHD at the start of their entrepreneurial journey, he rejects the myth of 'burning the boats'. "That isn't reality for 99% of us. Most people don't have the savings to risk it all. But you can dip your toe. Do an hour a day. Post in public. Test. Share. Build confidence. Focus on the 99% who want you to succeed, not the few who don't."

If he could speak to his teenage self, he'd tell him: "You're golden as you are. You might feel like a fish out of water most of your life, but one day this will all make sense. Trust me, it'll come good. Don't copy others. Don't twist yourself into shapes. Just be you."

Ryan Hopkins has a relentless energy, determination and is unapologetically himself. His ADHD has closed doors, opened others, broken his body, and built his career. He is obsessive, impatient, and sometimes extreme, but he is also determined, playful, ambitious, and utterly committed to changing the way we think about wellbeing.

What makes his story compelling is not the milestones along the way, but the conviction behind them; a refusal to shrink himself, a belief that difference can be a driver for change, and the courage to keep showing up long before anyone was listening. His vision is not simply about personal success, but about creating a world where wellbeing is understood, valued, and accessible to all.

Ryan's journey shows that the very traits once dismissed or misunderstood can become the spark for transformation, not just for one person, but for entire workplaces, communities, and futures.

Website: theryanhopkins.com
LinkedIn: @theryanhopkins
Instagram: @theryanhopkins1

Jeremy Didier

President of the Board of Directors for CHADD |
Licensed Social Worker | Licensed Addiction Counsellor
and ADHD-CCSP

She's said it in conference keynotes, in local support groups, and around her own kitchen table:

"Families like mine are not alone." For Jeremy Didier, it isn't a slogan — it's the throughline of her life, from growing up in a chaotic home to leading the board of CHADD.

Those words set the course for everything she does, from leading CHADD nationally to supporting families in her local community. A licensed clinical social worker (LSCSW), licensed addiction counsellor (LMAC), and ADHD-CCSP, she serves as President of the Board of Directors for CHADD, the leading US organisation for children and adults with ADHD.

She also co-coordinates Kansas City's local CHADD chapter, ADHDKC, continues to consult for ImpactParents where she began her coaching career, and trained extensively through both ADDCA and JST.

At every level, from local parent groups to national policy, Jeremy has channelled her personal and professional expertise into building systems that give families the recognition and support they deserve.

Jeremy grew up in the Midwest, the eldest of four children in a Catholic, upper-middle-class family. On the surface, it looked stable. Underneath, it was anything but. Both parents likely had undiagnosed ADHD, her mother lived with borderline personality disorder, and both were alcoholics. "Verbal and emotional abuse was common," she reflects. "And that left a mark."

She stood out in other ways, too. Tall from an early age, she's still 6ft now, with a traditionally male name and a late August birthday that made her the youngest in her class, she always felt out of step with her peers.

Yet academically, she thrived: straight A's, perfectionism, overachievement. "All the signs were there," Jeremy says. "On the inside, I was impulsive, risk-taking, emotionally flooded, and deeply uncomfortable in my own skin. But on the outside, it looked like I was doing great."

Her driving record, she jokes, was enough to terrify their family's insurance agent into a personal intervention. But there were glimpses of joy and freedom, too: she did drama, sang in the choir, and even had a short stint in modelling that took her to New York and Paris.

After earning her degree in broadcast journalism, Jeremy worked briefly as a reporter before following her husband Bryan, as his Navy career took them around the country. She later transitioned into telecom and pharmaceutical sales, where she achieved professional success but found personal stability elusive.

By then, their family was growing, and balancing the demands of young children with a high-pressure career added another layer of strain.

When the family eventually returned to Kansas City for Bryan to attend law school, Jeremy made the decision to step away from the corporate world and focus on raising their children. That choice marked a turning point and set the stage for the ADHD journey that would transform her life.

Their son Theo was diagnosed with ADHD at just three years old. "Suddenly, all the 'why is this so hard?' questions made sense," she recalls. Enrolling in a local ADHD Summer Treatment Program gave the family a lifeline. At a psychologist's suggestion, Jeremy started a CHADD chapter in Kansas City. Together with paediatrician Kristen, herself on an ADHD journey with her daughter, they founded ADHDKC.

The group quickly flourished, winning CHADD's Chapter of the Year award in its first year and sending Jeremy to her first national conference. There she met pioneers like Chris and Tommy Dendy, and Elaine Taylor-Klaus, who encouraged her to keep going. ADHDKC has since won multiple awards and become a cornerstone of support in the region.

Amid this, Jeremy faced her own turning point. At 36, sitting in a waiting room during Theo's neuropsych evaluation, she read an article by Dr Patricia Quinn. "It was like reading my own diary," she says. She turned to Bryan and admitted, "I think I have ADHD too." His response was instant: "Wait, you didn't know that already?"

The formal diagnosis was transformative. "It was like someone handed me a decoder ring for my entire life. I wasn't lazy or scattered, I had a neurodevelopmental condition that had gone undiagnosed for decades."

Paradoxically, she found it easier to hold things together while working full-time. The real breakdown came when she became a stay-at-home parent. "Five schedules, five lunches, five emotional needs every day — that's when things fell apart."

Alcohol had become a crutch, and Jeremy made the choice to stop drinking. She hasn't looked back since. "At the time, adult ADHD, especially in women, was almost never talked about. And if it was, no one admitted to being on medication. I started talking anyway."

From that moment on, Jeremy's professional path became inseparable from her ADHD journey. She trained formally as an ADHD coach through ADDCA and JST, began consulting with ImpactParents, and later qualified as a licensed clinical social worker and addiction counsellor.

Her combined expertise in ADHD, mental health, and addiction gave her a uniquely holistic perspective, one she has since carried into leadership roles, policy advocacy, and therapeutic practice.

At home, the challenges multiplied. Four of her five children have ADHD, with overlapping conditions including autism, dysgraphia, bipolar disorder, and Tourette syndrome. Her daughter Sophie's delayed diagnosis sharpened her focus on the overlooked presentation of ADHD in women and girls.

Her extended family's experience also shaped her advocacy. Both younger siblings were diagnosed with ADHD and bipolar disorder as teenagers, but by then, they had already turned to drugs and alcohol. Jeremy's sister later served jail time for a tragic alcohol-related accident and faced intense stigma and barriers to ADHD treatment on release.

"Her story is one of the reasons I fight so hard for justice-involved individuals," Jeremy explains. "When ADHD is missed in childhood, especially in marginalised communities, it becomes a fast track to school failure, addiction, and incarceration. I've seen it happen. And I won't stop pushing until mandated treatment and accommodations are the norm, not the exception. Families like mine are changing the story."

Ask Jeremy about her ADHD and she lights up. "I'm a connector. I build community like it's a superpower — probably because I spent my childhood scanning the emotional landscape to stay safe."

She describes herself as action-oriented, intuitive, and fast-moving. "I don't need things to be perfect before I start. That makes me an effective nonprofit leader. Momentum matters more than perfection."

Friends and colleagues describe her as passionate, energetic, and occasionally chaotic. She laughs at the truth in that. "I still double-book, forget appointments, or show up on the wrong day. But shoutout to stimulant medication — no speeding tickets since I started!"

The challenges are real too. Rejection sensitivity and self-esteem struggles are still part of her landscape. Money management has been another sticking point.

"My financial strategy used to be, ignore everything until it either expires, overdraws, or bursts into flames. I've evolved. Slightly." Relaxation is equally elusive: "My family jokes I'm incapable of sitting still at gatherings, which is not entirely untrue."

Jeremy credits ADHD with making her more compassionate, curious, and able to connect deeply with others. "People open up to me — I think ADHD gives me the kind of empathy that makes that possible." It has also opened professional doors she never expected. But she is clear about the costs. "The detail stuff — expense reports, taxes, paperwork. It's not just hard, it's soul-crushing. And I've made impulsive decisions that ended up being big mistakes. I'm learning to pause before leaping."

If she could change one aspect of her ADHD, it might be her impulsivity with money. If she could amplify one, it would be creative stamina. "Afternoon energy, please," she laughs. Her advice to others starting out is simple but powerful: "Keep going. It won't happen as quickly as you want it to, but it will happen. Find your people. Trust your gut. And don't wait until you feel ready — you probably never will."

To her younger self, she would say: "Don't panic. You're not broken. There's a name for what you're experiencing, and you're going to get help that makes life so much better. Oh, and maybe don't have five kids. Just kidding. Mostly."

Those who know Jeremy best describe her as high-energy, deeply empathetic, and unstoppable when she believes in a cause. Hyperfocus can take her deep into projects, but it is her ability to connect, to rally others, and to lead with conviction that truly sets her apart.

Her story is not only one of survival but of transformation — from a chaotic childhood to national leadership, from self-doubt to fierce advocacy. Above all, Jeremy Didier has built a life and career rooted in the belief she carries everywhere: Families like mine are changing the story.

Website: chadd.org
LinkedIn: @jeremy-didier-lscsw-lmac-adhd-ccsp-b17b2816

Dr Lynette Nusbacher

Founder Nusbacher & Associates | Strategy Advisor | Conservative Activist | NHS Deputy Chair & Senior Independent Director | Coach | Mentor | Current Affairs & History TV & Radio Broadcaster

Dr Lynette Nusbacher is a strategist in every sense of the word. A Doctor of Philosophy (D.Phil.), she is the Founder of Nusbacher & Associates, a trusted strategy advisor to leaders in business and government, a Conservative activist, an NHS Deputy Chair, and Senior Independent Director. She is also a coach, and mentor; as well as a familiar face, and voice, as a broadcaster on television, and radio, where she brings history, and current affairs to life with clarity, and insight.

For Lynette, strategy is both profession and purpose. "I practice strategy, not so much on my own behalf, but on others' behalf," she explains. That practice takes many forms. Coaching chief executives, serving on boards, advising on policy, and educating the wider public about the history and practice of strategy. Whether on the radio, television, or in boardrooms, it is all connected. Her mission is to help people understand what strategy is, and how to use it.

But her story doesn't begin in boardrooms or broadcasting studios. It begins in childhood, in a home where she was always told she had 'tremendous potential', whilst at the same time being accused of never living up to it. "I was often called the absent-minded professor," she recalls. "Very bright, but not punctual. Never got homework in on time. Nobody ever told me I was stupid, but the message was always that I wasn't working to my potential."

Family shaped Lynette's story as much as school ever did. She was adopted as a baby. She grew up with sisters, and from early on the differences between them were obvious. "One of the things that shaped my relationship with my parents was that I was unreliable, irresponsible and non-compliant as a child," she recalls. "That still shapes my relationship with my father and my stepmother. People close to me, including my parents, my sisters, my ex, my daughters, probably think that when I am unable to function in ways that I ought to, that it is constructive incompetence." Her parents, both very neurotypical, found it difficult to understand why some things felt impossible to her. Now as an adult, she shares, "My dad lives a long way away, and says why can't I just get a flight? Why can't I just turn up with my daughters? He finds it vexing that I haven't visited in a year. I think he's genuinely hurt by it, and I understand that my undiagnosed, untreated ADD makes that a factor."

Adoption itself added another layer, an early experience of rejection, that Lynette has come to see as inseparable from her later struggles with ADHD and rejection-sensitive dysphoria. "I've talked a lot about the extent to which being adopted interacts with having ADD, with rejection-sensitive dysphoria, and with that sense of being rejected by being put up for adoption. Nobody really talks about that. People talk about adoption as bringing in a child, but at its heart, it is also about a child being given away, rejected. That has been core to every single one of my relationships for my entire life."

Unlike many others in these pages, Lynette still doesn't have a formal ADHD diagnosis. She tried, more than once. Referred to her local adult ADD clinic in 2015, she went through assessments but quickly hit barriers. "One of the things I pointed out to the clinician was that I couldn't deal with post," she says. "If something came in a white window envelope, I just couldn't open it. The clinic agreed they'd mark their letters, so I'd know it was safe. But I forgot the marking. They kept sending those white window, threatening, envelopes, and eventually I stopped responding and the service discharged me."

Even now, despite being told she's 'top of the list', nothing has come through. And if it does, she may not open it. "That's how people like me get excluded," she says. "There's a tax on being neurodiverse. We pay late fees, we miss deadlines, we lose opportunities. For people already marginalised, it pushes them even further out."

The risks felt even bigger when a clinician warned her that an ADD diagnosis might have to be reported to the DVLA. "They said it could restrict my driving licence. So, the choice sounded like, walk out undiagnosed and drive freely, or get diagnosed and risk restriction. That's terrifying."

Lynette shares that for years, she was treated with SSRIs for anxiety and depression. "Looking back, my head exploded when I realised," she says. "I was on the wrong meds because I hadn't been properly diagnosed; I had undiagnosed ADD. Hundreds of thousands of people in this country are given antidepressants when what they really have is untreated ADHD. We're pumping SSRIs into people, at huge expense, and they're doing no good. And we say things like: 'We could never afford to medicate all the people with ADHD'. But we're already doing it. We're just using the wrong drugs."

That realisation was devastating, both personally, because of the years she lost, and professionally, because she knows as an economic historian what that means for society.

"The UK economy is stagnant in part because we exclude neurodiverse people from participating fully. We don't facilitate treatment; we gatekeep. The result? People end up on benefits, marginalised, unable to contribute at the level they could. We pay for it in productivity, in tax, in exclusion. It's not just a personal story, it's systemic."

Ask Lynette about success and she hesitates. "I struggle with that word," she admits. But after reflection, examples emerge.

She coached a first-time Chief Executive through the transition from consultancy into leadership. "I turned him from an excellent consultant into an excellent strategic leader," she says with quiet pride. She advised a law firm through Brexit, transforming their risk register from naïve to sophisticated. "The Times reported that law firm had experienced no surprises from Brexit. That was me."

During the pandemic, she led a project with one of the world's biggest law firms, guiding their board and executive committee to face the real post-pandemic future. "I told truth to power. At the time, I felt successful. Later, all I could think about was how dismissive the chief exec was of me and how, even to this day, I am still dealing with the tax liability. That's ADHD for you, wounded by the negatives and struggling to hold onto the positives."

Lynette struggles to frame ADHD as a strength. The challenges are easier to name; object permanence, difficulty maintaining relationships, financial management and above all, rejection-sensitive dysphoria. "That has shaped my life for almost 60 years," she says. "It affects work, relationships, everything."

There are creative strengths too. She's a skilled calligrapher and has often found herself immersed in arts and crafts, woodwork, even darning socks. "Calligraphy is precise, focused, it's a great rabbit hole for ADHD," she reflects. "It's mindfulness for me, even if I haven't always recognised it."

But the bigger story is how others perceive her. At work, she is seen as "immensely competent, intelligent, charismatic." It's professionally useful, but some of it is also a mask. "When my ADHD shows up, when I'm too intense, or focused on the wrong thing, it's not seen as quirky or enthusiastic. It's seen as manipulative or Machiavellian."

That perception has hurt her personally, too. Unmanaged ADHD contributed to the breakdown of her marriage. Family members sometimes dismiss her difficulties too.

Behind the mask, the cost of 'passing' as competent is enormous. "People think I'm far more together than I am, because I have to be," she admits. "Otherwise, I couldn't function as a director or a professional. But the truth is, almost every job I've left, I've left because of the challenges of my neurodivergence."

Professionally, ADHD has made pitching work, applying for jobs, following up with clients, and managing money immensely difficult. "Silence feels like rejection," she says. "I believe it, I assume I'm being rejected, and then I don't follow up."

She's learned to survive with support: body doubling, executive assistance, and accountability. "Even statutory training or expenses wouldn't get done otherwise," she admits. But there are moments of brilliance too, in lectures, TV appearances, or coaching sessions, where her focus becomes a gift.

If she could change one thing, it would be rejection-sensitive dysphoria. "It has shaped my personal and professional life more than anything else," she says.

And if she could give advice to someone starting their own business journey? "Self-knowledge will be your greatest asset. Know what you're good at, what you need help with, and what you cannot do without facilitation. That awareness will help you function better everywhere — work, home, relationships."

If Lynette could speak to her 10 or 15-year-old self, she knows what she would say:
"You already know your brain is different. Your mission is to spend your life understanding those differences, respecting the pros and cons, and crafting your life to meet your needs, not someone else's."

She draws a striking parallel with LGBTQIA+ communities, where people are often asked the same question. For years, the easy answer was 'it gets better'. But that shifted. "We don't say that now, because we can't promise it," she explains. "Instead, the message has become: 'Don't listen to what people say. Who you think you are, really is who you are. Live accordingly."

For Lynette, the neurodivergence version of that is even deeper. "It touches every corner of your life, public and private. And in my case, adoption made it even more profound."

So, her message to her younger self is simple but powerful: "Who you think you are, matters. The person you know yourself to be is real. Don't let anyone tell you otherwise. Build a life that fits you. You won't thrive forcing yourself to fit someone else's mould."

Against the weight of rejection, misdiagnosis, and misunderstanding, what makes Lynette remarkable is not just her achievements, but the way she has woven struggle, identity, and strategy into a life lived on her own terms. In that, she offers a quiet lesson in courage and, in doing so, shows others what is possible.

Website: nusbacher.com
LinkedIn: @nusbacher
Instagram: @lynettenusbacher

Nick Conn

Founder & CEO at Help4Addiction and Rehubs | Author

Nicholas Conn knows what it feels like to lose everything, and what it takes to rebuild from nothing. Today, he is the CEO of Help 4 Addiction, and the founder of Rehubs, an award-winning online rehab programme achieving better outcomes than many residential clinics. But long before the success, his story was one of chaos, self-doubt, and survival.

"I was doing 8 grams of cocaine a day," Nick says quietly. "About £400 a day. I ended up homeless in Berlin, with the Albanian mafia after me. That's where my life took me."

It's a long way from the family home he grew up in, a boy with 'amazing parents' and what he calls a great childhood. Yet beneath the surface, there was always a mismatch. "I was a right-handed person in a left-handed person's world," he says. "I just couldn't do school the way other people did it."

He remembers one moment vividly. "A teacher was explaining something, I was gone in my head. As soon as he finished, I asked a question. It was exactly what he'd just answered. Everyone laughed. From then on, I had this fear of asking questions. It took me years to undo."

Not knowing what else to do, Nick followed his brother into the police. At Hendon, where trainees lived on site for 18 weeks, the pressure was relentless. Recruits had to hit 80% every week or be kicked out. "I was struggling," he says. "Then I was introduced to cocaine. Suddenly, I was getting 95, 96%. I was retaining information, flying through. I thought I'd cracked it."

But what began as a lifeline became a trap. Nick left the police, drifted deeper into addiction, and ended up in Berlin, running drugs for organised crime. "Homeless, completely gone," he says. "That was me."

The turning point came with a phone call home. "I told my family, 'I've got a huge drug problem, I'm homeless, I've got the mafia after me'. They told me to go to a hotel, call them from there. They paid for the room over the phone. I had the best shower of my life. They flew me home the next day."

Even then, recovery wasn't simple. "We tried to find a rehab; it was almost impossible. No prices listed, the only place anyone knew was the Priory at £25,000. Eventually, through one of my dad's contacts, we found one in Bognor Regis. I thought I'd hit rock bottom being homeless. Then I hit rehab in Bognor Regis."

He stayed for three months. Relapsed. Tried again. "Rehab is a bubble," he says. "Anyone can stay clean in there. It's when you come out that's the challenge."

Eventually, he found his footing. A year into recovery, he opened a spreadsheet. "I thought, who else is struggling to find a rehab? I listed every rehab I could find in the country, location, prices, modalities, detox, and waiting times. That Excel sheet became Help 4 Addiction. It grew into one of the largest private addiction services in the UK."

But many people were still shut out: parents with children, people who couldn't afford it, carers, those tied to jobs. "There was nothing for them. So, I set up Rehubs." He raised £1 million, brought in

Professor Spada, one of the world's most cited addiction scientists, and built a programme that now outperforms many traditional clinics. "I actually had the idea 12 years ago," he admits. "It was too early. COVID made it possible. Now it works." He smiles. "I won Innovator of the Year last year for Rehubs. That's the one thing I'd put my name next to."

By the time his first child was born, Nick had been clean for several years and was running his business. But when fatherhood hit, so did something unexpected. "I suffered with postnatal depression, I didn't even know men could get that. I was embarrassed to talk about it. When I did, other men reached out to me. That was powerful."

Parenting exposed something else, too. "I really struggled with the baby stage. Remembering bottles, routines, all of it. My wife is incredibly structured. For her, it was water off a duck's back. For me, it was overwhelming." He spoke to a friend, a psychiatrist who specialised in ADHD. "He said, 'Why don't you have an assessment?' Four hours later, which is ironic, expecting someone with ADHD to sit through four hours of questions, I was diagnosed."

Medication wasn't the answer. "Because of my addiction history, it was horrible. I got the comedown without the high. My brain started telling me to take more than prescribed. As soon as that happened, I stopped." Instead, Nick relies on the people around him. "I employ brilliant staff, I delegate, I've got a great wife. Between them, they basically manage my life. That's how I cope."

For Nick, ADHD is both an engine and a weight. "It can be a superpower," he says, "but it also kills your confidence." The superpowers are clear: creativity, innovation, and hyperfocus. "I love problems. I love finding solutions. I can sit and obsess until it's done." But the challenges are constant. "Organisation is the hardest thing. I leave things late, then expect my team to drop everything. My timelines are unrealistic. My impulsivity drives everyone mad."

His wife sees it up close. "She'd say I'm a liability. She'll ask for a shelf and I'll buy a £1000 drill set and a laser level, then pay someone else to put it up. I get fixated. I forget plans. I can come across as selfish. But she's very understanding."

At work, the story is similar. "My heart is good, but my execution is bad," Nick admits. "I expect people to work at the speed I do when I'm hyper-focused. It's not realistic. That can give me a bad reputation." Recently, he hired a Head of Service. "He's the opposite of me. He fills the gaps, manages the team, and makes people happier. He's like a buffer. It works."

The view from his team and family is not all frustration. They see the loyalty, the care, and the creativity that drives him. "I'm not hierarchical," he says. "I value my people. I'd do anything for them. But my poor organisation makes life harder for them. I know that."

At home, his wife experiences the intensity as much as the love. "If I'm sending a work message and she talks to me, I lose my temper. I can't multitask. She can. It causes friction. But she knows I'd do anything for her and the kids."
Parenting has sharpened his perspective. "I don't tell my kids, 'That's amazing,' when they show me their drawings. I ask, 'What do you think?' I want them to learn internal validation. That's what I

missed growing up, always questioning myself, always searching outside for confidence."

Their school helps too. "It's so inclusive. No Edwardian-style teaching. They'll go outside, make a bonfire, and cook chapatis in religious education. My kids retain so much. It shows how much the environment matters for neurodivergent children."

If he could change one thing about his ADHD, Nick knows what it would be. "Organisation. It affects everything. I'd be calmer, and less erratic if I had it."

And if others could change something about him? "They'd probably say my impulsivity and my timelines. They'd say my heart is good, but my execution is bad. And they'd be right."

Asked what he would tell his younger self, he doesn't hesitate. "Believe in yourself. Back yourself. A big part of my cocaine addiction was low self-esteem. Cocaine gave me the euphoria, and confidence I was always searching for. I'd tell that boy to trust in his passions."

For others starting their entrepreneurial journey with ADHD, his advice is pragmatic. "Invest in organisational systems early. You need structures that fit your brain. I always say it's like needing a Stacey Solomon closet organiser, but for life."

Nick Conn's life has been shaped by extremes, from the highs of hyperfocus to the lows of addiction, from sleeping rough in Berlin, to winning Innovator of the Year. In June 2025, he also achieved another success, releasing his first book on Amazon: White Lines and Blue Lights: A True Story of Addiction, Survival, and Redemption from a Former Cop, not just a memoir, but a survival guide for anyone in the depths of despair trying to find their way through. What threads everything together though, is his refusal to stop building, even when confidence wavers.

"I feel like a swan," he says. "Elegant on the surface, paddling like hell underneath."

The truth is that the paddling has powered something extraordinary. Nick has turned his hardest challenges into solutions for others. The boy who once feared asking questions now leads one of the UK's most innovative addiction services. His legacy is not just in the businesses he's built, but in the hope he offers to those who think they're too broken to succeed.

Because Nick knows better than most: even when the world writes you off, there is always a way back.

Website:	help4addiction.co.uk
Book:	White Lines and Blue Lights
LinkedIn:	nicholas-conn-9a032343
Instagram:	@dadinrecovery

Elizabeth Hutton OBE

CEO at Kicks Count

Elizabeth Hutton's son Toby, born sleeping, didn't live to see the world, yet he changed the course of his mother's life, and countless others. His story is now at the heart of a movement that has saved babies across the UK, and beyond.

Today, Elizabeth is CEO of Kicks Count, the country's leading awareness charity for baby movements in pregnancy. Her story weaves together grief, resilience, ADHD, and the fire to act when others might hold back. "Everything I've done with Kicks Count is because of him," she says. "He's at the heart of all of it. It's pride. It's his legacy as much as mine."

That legacy became her anchor. Out of the silence of loss came a voice that reached Parliament, the press, and parents everywhere. In 2024, Elizabeth was awarded an OBE for her services to education and prevention of stillbirth. For her, the honour was not about her it was all about Toby. His legacy: seen, valued, and lasting.

Elizabeth describes her early years with a mix of humour, and warmth. She grew up in Basingstoke until, at age 10, her family moved to Singapore for her father's work. Where most children might have been anxious, she was exhilarated. "I didn't find it daunting at all. I just found it really exciting. I was going to a new school, meeting new people, and I loved the idea of it. My only worry was not finding out what was going to happen on Neighbours. My best friend promised to write to me every week and update me."

The international school she attended was full of expat children whose families came and went on short contracts. "Friendships were disjointed, but I didn't struggle with that. It was always interesting to me. I think having that disjointedness actually helped me."

Academically, she stood out. "My nickname was the Jammy Dodger, because I never seemed to revise or work, but always did well. My geography teacher finally said, 'I don't want you doing any more homework. It's rubbish. I can tell you've done it on the bus, but you'll ace the exam anyway. Let's not waste our time.' She really saw what I needed."

She was endlessly talkative, her energy spilling over into classrooms. Teachers were exasperated, but also fond of her. Her younger sister, three years below, would always hear, 'Oh no, Elizabeth's sister, not another one'. Still, Elizabeth always got the grades she needed.

At 18, she returned to England to study retail management at university, convinced she would one day open a coffee shop. "I knew exactly what it was going to be. Then halfway through I went, nah, I want to go into childcare. I really wanted a baby."

She became a nursery nurse, then, with typical audacity, applied for a manager's role. "I didn't have the qualifications, but I blagged it. I was studying for the same qualifications as the nursery nurses I was managing. It was a bit odd."

Two years later, bored again, she quit and fell into an admin role with the police where she stayed for 7 years. It was during that time that her rollercoaster journey into parenthood began. She gave birth to her daughter, Toby was born sleeping, and then later, her rainbow baby boy was born.

On maternity leave with her youngest son, Elizabeth began looking for ways to prevent other families from experiencing the same heartbreak that her family had endured. She found a charity called 'Count the Kicks' on Twitter and started volunteering. What began as small tasks soon became the work of her life.

From the start, Elizabeth's ADHD traits shaped how she led. "The biggest strength is the impulsivity," she says. "Having an idea and acting on it without talking myself out of it. Messaging an MP to ask them to take a bill through Parliament. Messaging Holly Willoughby. Just doing it. No 'what if they say no' - just wing it and see."

It worked. Surprise Surprise featured Kicks Count in a national campaign fronted by Holly Willoughby and Alesha Dixon. Orders for wristbands exploded overnight. "It went from zero to 100 in a day," she recalls. "I loved that buzz."

Her proudest moment came with the Doppler bill. Home Dopplers, handheld devices that allow pregnant women to listen to a baby's heartbeat, were being sold by many major retailers. Elizabeth knew the risks. "If you saw someone collapse in the street, would you check their pulse and walk away? Or would you call an ambulance? That was my analogy, and it worked. Hearing a heartbeat doesn't mean your baby is healthy. We got it debated in Parliament, got Tesco and Mothercare to stop selling them, and got a government review. People still tell me my own analogy back to me now. That was one of my biggest successes, and I hope, one that has prevented more baby losses."

Like many with ADHD, Elizabeth works in bursts. "I tell the trustees, don't look at what I achieve in a day or week. Look at six months.

What I do in those bursts is more than most people achieve consistently. Then I crash. You just have to ride it out because I'll come back with fire."

That pattern extends to her many side hustles. "I set up businesses selling candles, sweets, Taylor Swift prints, and garden designs. Every time I'd spend £2,000, 3 months later I had £2,000 of unsold stock in the garage. I started calling everything 'Sienna Burlington'. Sienna was a name I liked; Burlington sounded posh. So, everything became Sienna Burlington. It's a running joke now. But I wish I'd thought of it earlier, then it could all have sat under one umbrella."

Elizabeth's formal diagnosis came through her son. "He was struggling in school. While filling out his assessment sheets, I realised I was describing myself."

She had suspected ADHD for years and a book about ADHD in women cemented it. "I read paragraphs to my sister," she said. "That's you. That book could have been written about you."

Still, she hesitated. After surviving breast cancer in 2016, and entering menopause at 37 following surgery, her mental health plummeted. "People kept telling me it was menopause brain fog. But I knew it wasn't. I wasn't getting any of the good sides of ADHD anymore, just the flatness."

She went to the GP and was referred but was told a diagnosis would take years. On a trip to Singapore, a school friend pushed her. "She said, 'Why can't you go private?' It hadn't even occurred to me. I got back, booked a psychiatrist, and within a week and a half, I had my diagnosis."

The relief was enormous. "Before that I felt like I was only getting the negatives, no positives, no hyperfocus, no fire. The diagnosis, and medication gave me that balance back."

Elizabeth's impulsivity remains her greatest strength. "When I got the breast cancer diagnosis, it wasn't just shock. It was, 'right, now I've got something to fight'. That adrenaline kicks in."
But finishing is harder. "Hardly any job in my house is finished. I'll paint the walls but not the skirting. I need people like Lisa, who worked with me for years, or my friend Karen. They're finishers. They tie up the loose ends I leave behind."

Family find it frustrating, her daughter especially, rolling her eyes at yet another round of redecorating. But they also see her fire. Trustees at Kicks Count know that after every lull, she'll return with energy, and ideas that change everything.

The charity has helped save countless babies, and for Elizabeth, that's what it was always about. There have been many things she's proud of, but this for her is the thing that means the most. "When people say, 'My baby wouldn't be here without Kicks Count', that's it. That's the achievement. That's what matters." Recognition followed. In 2024, Elizabeth received the letter that would change her forever. "When I opened it and saw I was being awarded an OBE, I thought it was a wind-up," she laughs. "I couldn't believe it. I don't see myself as someone who gets things like that. I just wanted to stop other families from going through what we did."

On the day she received her OBE, Elizabeth's journey home took her past the crematorium where Toby is buried. She stopped, took the medal from its box, and placed it by his grave. "I hadn't planned it, but it felt right," she says. "I thought, this is because of you. Kicks Count is your legacy as much as mine. I wouldn't have stuck with it without you."

Elizabeth also recognises the power of celebrity influence. "When Holly Willoughby fronted our poster campaign, orders went through the roof. Babies were saved. I told her it was because of her. She said, "No, you did the work." She underestimates it. Five minutes of her time saved so many lives.

But it can go the other way. A well-known celebrity with 1.4 million followers said that reduced movement at the end of pregnancy was normal. I was horrified. Luckily, followers corrected her and pointed people to us. The ripple effect works both ways."

Her advice to entrepreneurs with ADHD is direct. "Give it a go. What's the worst that can happen? Maybe start smaller than you think, don't buy thousands of products up front. And keep your business name generic, so it can flex. Don't pigeonhole yourself."

If she could speak to her younger self, she'd keep it simple. "You've got ADHD. What you think are obsessions are hyperfocus. They won't last forever. Embrace it. You'll be alright."

Elizabeth Hutton's story is one of fire: the fire of grief, the fire of impulsive action, the fire of ideas that won't wait. She has turned that fire into impact, saving lives, and reshaping national conversations.

"I wouldn't change what we went through," she says softly. "It was horrible at the time, but it gave me Kicks Count. It gave me pride.

And it gave me him, Toby. That's what I come back to every time, more than medals, honours, or success, it's his legacy that endures.

Website: www.kickscount.org.uk
LinkedIn: @ehutton1
Instagram: @elizabeth_kickscount

Rebecca Whelan

Medical Director at ADHD 360

Rebecca Whelan has built her career on clarity in the toughest of moments. Now the Medical Director at ADHD 360, with over two decades as a mental health nurse, she is known for bringing calm to chaos.

"I got quite badly abused by one of the teachers from 13-15 years old. He picked up on my vulnerability, groomed me for years and took away a lot of my childhood and innocence. He went to prison for 5 years when I was 15. But at the time, the teachers were more-or-less on his side. I was scapegoated. People talked about me, laughed and didn't want to be around me. It was made out as though it was my fault, which I believed for a long time."

She buried herself in study. "I had nothing else and was miserable, so I thought the only way to make things better was to show my worth through results. I got really good GCSEs and that feedback I'd done well was enough to make me feel less ashamed of myself."

After school, Rebecca headed to university but only lasted a week. Communal living left her feeling exposed and anxious, so she came home. Her mum was blunt: "You're not sitting round this house listening to The Smiths all day." Rebecca's reply was just as firm: "I'm not, I'm going to be a nurse."

Nursing hadn't been her first choice; she'd wanted to write, to do journalism, but it became her redemption. It pleased her mum and gave her purpose. On the wards, with patients from every walk of life, she thrived. "I loved people, loved feeling I was doing something for others."

Her career, she says, found her. Acute mental health became her home for twenty years. "I've honestly never woken up and thought 'I've got to go to work today.' Most people burn out after 2 or 3 years. I never did. The drama, the risk, the critical thinking, it all played into my strengths."

But if work was stable, life outside it rarely was. She moved house on impulse, her children going to five different primary schools through childhood. "If work was steady, home was chaos; if home was steady, work was chaos."

Rebecca was with her first partner, a woman, for 13 years, and together they had her first two children. "I wish I'd been able to see things more clearly then. I regret how it ended. But I was impulsive and unsettled and I thought I was chasing something else."

Later, Rebecca married her husband, also a nurse. Their relationship was intense but unsafe, marked by alcohol problems, social services involvement, and domestic abuse. "It was frightening and chaotic, but I knew I had to protect myself and my children," she says. Not long afterwards, he died, leaving Rebecca a widow with three young children, the youngest just two years old.

Rather than pause, she pushed forward. She began a Masters, determined to prove she could provide for her family. "I needed a distraction, and to show I could be self-sufficient, especially for my children," she explains.

Through it all, crisis sharpened her focus. "My best thinking has always come in crisis. That's when my thoughts are clearest and I can manage everyone else's emotions while staying calm."

It was only later, working alongside her friend and colleague, the late Dave Scarrott, that things began to make sense. Dave wasn't just a teammate; he became a mentor and a constant presence, someone who pushed her to see what she couldn't yet see in herself.

With his encouragement, she left the NHS and moved to ADHD 360 with him, and it was there, surrounded by patients whose stories mirrored her own, that she felt a jolt of recognition. "I remember thinking: I've got ADHD. It was that lightbulb moment, everything made sense."

Soon after, she asked to be assessed by then-Clinical Director Lisa Mangle. "She said, 'This is the most classic combined type I've seen.' Around the same time my son was diagnosed, he's very similar to me." The diagnosis reframed her life. "Before that, I didn't trust my own judgement. With the diagnosis, I realised it wasn't that I was a bad person. It was impulsivity. If I stop and reflect before deciding, I make better decisions."

Through ADHD 360, Rebecca was asked to appear on the TV show, *Loose Women,* to talk about ADHD. For someone who had spent her life avoiding attention, it was a terrifying step. "That's been one of the biggest barriers for me to overcome," she admits. "I never liked the spotlight. At school, I went red answering the register. And suddenly, there I was, being asked to sit on *Loose Women*, talking about ADHD in front of the nation. The aftermath was huge, it was overwhelming."

It was unthinkable for someone who had previously struggled with basic training exercises. "Two years ago, I couldn't even do a 'train the trainer' exercise without getting convoluted and losing people. My brain runs four simultaneous thoughts at once, and that comes out verbally, which isn't good for teaching. To then be on live TV felt impossible. But it forced me to grow."

That growth came with encouragement from those around her. "At first I wanted to shy away, but Phil [Anderton] pushed me," she says. Today, Rebecca leads the ADHD 360 Academy, where she teaches new clinicians from scratch. "Every month, I stand up, teach new clinicians who know nothing about ADHD diagnostics, everything they need so they can safely be in front of patients. It's a huge responsibility."

Public speaking, once unthinkable, has become part of her identity. "Now people say to me, 'I want to be as good as you at presenting.' That's the biggest compliment because I never saw myself like that. Two years ago, I'd have said no way. And now I actually look forward to it." For Rebecca, the Academy is more than a role; it's her legacy. "It belongs to me. I feel responsible for it. It's passing on the knowledge in a meaningful way, ensuring learning is strong enough that patients are safe. If I could be remembered for one thing, it would be that."

Rebecca describes her ADHD as both a strength and a burden. In her professional life, it gives her an edge. "I do my best thinking in crisis. At work, in trauma, in grief, my thoughts are clearest then. I can manage everybody else's emotions and stay calm. I can't ever imagine doing nothing. I need productivity, purpose, and achievement every day. Despite all the struggles in my life, I've never lost passion for my job. The outcome for patients is always the driver."

But that clarity doesn't always carry into her personal world. "The balance is never right. At work, I can be excellent, but at home, I miss parents' evenings, payments, and practical stuff. My car got clamped because I forgot to tax it. My son missed a Barcelona trip because I hadn't checked the passport emails." Dates and details often slip through. "I forget anniversaries, birthdays. Even the anniversary of my dad's death, 10 years, I didn't remember until someone posted on Facebook. It's not because I don't care; I care deeply. But my brain doesn't retain certain things. Numbers, dates, detail – gone."

Memories are another gap. "My kids say, 'Do you remember when?' and I just don't. Family members can remember things about my life that I can't. I wonder if it's ADHD, trauma or just my brain being too full."

At work, however, she feels celebrated for the very traits she once saw as flaws. "My deputy, Lisa, champions me. She says, 'I love the way your brain works.' That makes me emotional because nobody's ever said that before. They see me as an ideas person, lots of ideas, but we have to channel them into results."

Home life brings a different kind of understanding. "My dad had ADHD, my sisters too. My children are neurodiverse. So, we're all in our own bubble and it feels normal to us. Outside that, I know I'm not easy to live with." Her relationship with her partner has brought stability. "With him, I feel seen and loved for exactly who I am. There's no pretence. We understand each other in a way I never had before, compassionate towards how each of us experiences life. After everything, to have that love and acceptance is something I don't take for granted."

When she reflects on ADHD, Rebecca is clear-eyed about both sides. If she could change one thing, it would be impulsivity and inattentiveness to loved ones because its caused the most chaos, her inattentiveness and forgetfulness around important dates, anniversaries etc. But she would also amplify what works. "When dopamine is high, my thoughts are sharp and articulate. I'd love to channel that all the time, not just in crisis."

Her message to others is encouragement. "Believe ADHD is an asset, not a problem. You'll think differently, work differently, bring ideas others won't. Surround yourself with people who understand your brain and can help you channel it. With the right support, you can achieve more than you think."

And to her younger self: "You're not a bad person. You're not broken. The way your brain works will make sense one day and will become your strength. Don't let the shame or blame define you."

Rebecca's life has been a pendulum, swinging between stability and chaos, between achievement and upheaval. She's moved house on impulse, adopted more dogs than she can count, lived through long-term love, regret, abuse, widowhood, loss and finally, acceptance. From a young girl who fought to prove her worth, to a leader trusted to shape the future of ADHD services, Rebecca has turned survival into purpose and purpose into legacy.

Website: www.adhd-360.com
LinkedIn: @rebecca-whelan-06a8a0181

Adam Dance, MP

Member of Parliament

At just 33, Adam Dance serves as the Liberal Democrat Member of Parliament for Yeovil. It's a role many spend decades building towards, yet Adam's route here was anything but conventional. From the boy labelled "naughty" and publicly shamed by teachers when he needed to take his ADHD medication at school, to the teenager whose blazer was set alight by bullies, his story is one of resilience forged early, and fuelled by a determination to prove there was always more to him than the labels suggested.

Having ADHD and dyslexia, Adam found school could be a daily battle. He was known as the child who couldn't sit still, who spent almost as much time outside lessons as in them. "If I couldn't spell a word, my ADHD would flare. It felt like a fire in my belly, and I'd have what I called explosion moments."

Adam shares that whilst school was hard, and there was a distinct lack of support and understanding, he was fortunate to have some teachers who did have his back and believed in him, - one of whom now works alongside him in his parliamentary office. But even that support was tempered by the daily reality of relentless bullying from fellow students.

Taking medication at set times became a public humiliation when a teacher announced in front of the class, "Time you go and take your pill now, Adam". What should have been treatment instead became a label, leaving him exposed to taunts and cruel words from classmates, made worse by the lack of support and empathy from the very teachers who should have protected him.

At fifteen, things escalated. Another student set his blazer on fire as he got off the bus. For Adam, it was a turning point. "If I'd gone home, my dad would have told me to fight back. But that wasn't me. So, I went to the local youth centre instead."

That youth club became a lifeline. When funding cuts closed youth provision, Adam channelled his anger into action. "If it wasn't for that youth club, I'd probably be in prison now or dead because I'd have taken my own life." Instead, he joined the youth parish council, became chair, and helped reinstate a youth club in his village.

By eighteen, Adam was already carving out his own path. Convinced that his ADHD prevented him from working for anyone else, he set up a landscaping business. "Looking back, I don't know how I did it on my own. I just kept going." That business kept him afloat for more than a decade, until he finally shut it down to focus entirely on politics.

Politics, at first, wasn't on the cards for him. He studied brickwork to mask his sexuality, trying to blend in by doing something "masculine," but found himself drawn back to horticulture. Alongside work and study, Adam stayed involved in local councils, frustrated by what he saw as ineffective leadership. "I thought, 'If he can do it, I can do it better.'"

Mentored by figures like Paddy Ashdown, he eventually stood for the district council in 2013, winning the election in 2015 at just 22. By 2019, he'd been re-elected, and by 2022, he was Somerset's Cabinet Member for Public Health, Equality and Diversity. The step up to Westminster came next.

Adam was diagnosed with ADHD at six or seven, though he only revisited his medical records years later when Parliament needed evidence to provide support. The experience was jarring. "The notes said I'd hidden under a desk at the appointment, refused to come out, even bitten a doctor's finger. Reading that back was traumatic." Medication brought mixed results. "Mum said it made me a zombie. I stopped at 16. The pills were a trigger, they reminded me of bullying, of feeling wound up more, not less."

Asked to describe his ADHD, Adam points to both the drive and the friction it creates. Thinking about the strengths, "It gives me get-up-and-go. I never switch off. That means I get things done." The challenges, however, are harder, "Anxiety. Constant overthinking. I can snap if too much builds up, though I've learned to control it. And I always doubt myself, even with big wins, I always question if I'm good enough."

Rejection sensitivity is part of the picture too. "Put me in front of a thousand people and I'll speak confidently. Put me in a party where I don't know anyone, and I'll be the quiet one in the corner. I replay conversations, worrying if I said the wrong thing. It's exhausting."

Chrissy, who has known Adam for years – first as friends and more recently, she has stepped into the role of his PA, describes him affectionately and honestly, "He's 100 miles an hour. He can listen to three conversations at once. Sometimes unpredictable, with the odd mood wobble, and he takes things to heart, but people would also call it his superpower."

From a professional perspective, she sees strengths that Adam doesn't always recognise. "He's a people pleaser, which means he gives great service to constituents. He gets overwhelmed sometimes, but he's learned to take five minutes out and then come back stronger. He's approachable and empathic, and people stop him in the street constantly. That warmth is rare in politics. Everyone wants to talk to him."

She adds: "On low days, I'd remind him how many people admire him. We can't walk down the street or go for dinner without people coming up to him, wanting to talk to him or thanking him. He doesn't always see it, but they do."

When asked what he's most proud of, Adam names two things: the landscaping business he built from scratch at 18 and becoming an MP as a neurodivergent man. One moment in particular stays with him: "We went to a school recently, primary school, and a boy asked if they could talk to us after. He explained to me that he has ADHD and dyslexia and told me, 'You've made me realise I won't fail in life'. That meant everything and is why I do what I do."

We asked Adam what advice he would give someone newly diagnosed or struggling? "Focus on the positives. Don't hide it. Be yourself. The minute you hide it; you're not being your authentic self."

And to his younger self, the boy standing at the bus stop with his blazer on fire? "Your future is bright. Keep going. Don't listen to the haters. Be yourself."

Adam doesn't frame his ADHD as a badge of success or a neat story of triumph. It has been messy, complicated, and painful at times. He is still, in many ways, the boy at the bus stop who just wanted to be accepted. The difference now is that he uses that same fire to fight for others, not through fists, but through voice and action.

And while his seat in Parliament at 33 is remarkable, it isn't the title that defines him. It's the way people gravitate towards him, from the primary school visits helping neurodivergent children to feel seen or the people stopping him in the street to thank him, opening up to him in moments of need, or simply wanting to connect. That warmth and openness is what he carries closest to his heart, and what makes his journey less about politics and far more about people.

Website: www.yeovil-libdems.org.uk
LinkedIn: @adam-dance
Instagram: @adam4yeovil

CHAPTER 5

The Familiar Faces*

*
These are the people you might already recognise, names you have seen in the media, on stage or on your screens. They have built public profiles while carving out their own unique paths in business and beyond. Behind the visibility and the life portrayed in the public eye, their stories reveal grit, resilience, and the same determination to succeed that runs through every chapter of this book.

Nadia Essex

Director at Kidfluence | Author | Dating Coach | TV Personality

UNSTOPPABLE BY DESIGN

272

Who is Nadia Essex? At first glance and from her TV appearances as a well-known Celebrity Dating Coach, she is polished, confident, in her words, "Tits and Teeth", and very much in her element surrounded by the glitz and glamour of the celebrity world and the cocktail bars of Chelsea. In real life, though, she is a private person.

She's a mum, a professional, a late-to-the-party ADHDer going on her journey of diagnosis, an advocate for women, and an extremely passionate, professional, and credible business owner forging a successful path in the world of influencer marketing.

But behind the fame and the character Nadia has 'played' in the past, her story has been shaped by high highs and lower lows. Her journey is one from privilege to poverty, from celebrity fame to a rock bottom collapse. At its core, Nadia's story is one of resilience, rediscovery, and grace.

As a child, Nadia remembers her life always felt like a rollercoaster. Early on, things were privileged and idyllic. She went to private school, had horse riding lessons, the family had extravagant holidays to Disney World, and her life was peaceful, calm and without worry.

Later, Nadia's whole world came crashing down when her parents divorced, her father's businesses folded, and her family lost everything overnight. She found herself going from a comfortable and privileged style of living to social housing. She was taken out of private school and moved to a state school, and her life was now shaped by fear and worry for how their family would financially survive.

At 14, this experience of extremes taught Nadia that she wanted to be independent – both personally and financially. She remembers her first Saturday job in a bakery and the thrill she got using her pay packet to go and buy herself a ring from the Argos catalogue. That thrill of providing for herself gave her a huge boost. She felt free.

That sense of freedom has never left her. Nadia opted not to go to university and instead threw herself into the world of work. Initially, she worked in sales where there was a natural fast pace, the ability to make lots of money and her success was because of her natural charm and ability. She found it exciting at first but then grew bored.

She then job-hopped for a few years, initially finding the new job exciting but then feeling restless and bored and eventually moving on.

This pattern continued until Nadia was in her 20s. She moved into the corporate world, working on Oxford Street, selling marketing services. She stayed in this role for two years but eventually hit burnout. She experienced anxiety at the thought of returning to this world and so quit, took a sabbatical, and began experimenting. Something she now realises was her brain's way of looking for excitement, looking for dopamine, looking for a place where she could fit. Nadia was always full of ideas and was not afraid to think outside the box. She thought about starting a nursery or a concierge service – ultimately looking for the next thing that might make her financially independent and successful.

The journey her career took next came completely out of the blue. An ex-boss that she had stayed in contact with got divorced and called Nadia asking her to come on a night out and be her 'wing-woman'. This became the first of many 'wing-woman' nights out and she realised, she was good at it. She had a natural ability to help match-make. Word spread and soon people were asking if they could book her to help them go on dates and find 'the one'.

Throughout this, Nadia had developed an interest in going on TV. She appeared on First Dates, and this fuelled her desire even more. She loved it and she felt she'd found her calling.

As with everything Nadia has ever done in her professional career, she put her all into it. She hustled, she pitched, she grafted. She pitched herself as the UK's answer to the Millionaire Matchmaker. She continued to network, she would go to places she knew celebrities went to, she made friends with paparazzi, and posted constantly on social media, pitching her skills as a matchmaker.

Then, her career-defining moment came. She got a call for a screen test from Channel 4 and suddenly, the relentless determination and the hard graft she had put in had all been worth it. She landed the role as Celebrity Dating Coach where she would spend the next two years matchmaking for single celebs.

She had made it. She had landed her dream role. On the surface, this was everything she had ever wanted, everything she had worked towards. She was on TV, she was in the public eye, she was credible, and she was celebrated. She was at the peak of her career. Beneath that outward fame and success, though, was another reality. Nadia says, "It was my best job and my worst nightmare".

She explains she felt fulfilled but broken at the same time. She was lonely, had no money and was being harassed daily by bailiffs for not paying bills on time, yet her evenings would be spent glammed up at red carpet events – a far cry from the negotiation and stress she was experiencing at home during the day. It was a brutal, unforgiving industry and a duty of care was lacking. She eventually left the show in 2018 when she hit rock bottom. She found herself homeless, hopeless, and ended up living in a friend's walk-in wardrobe. She had also just found out that she was pregnant.

Falling pregnant became her catalyst to pick herself up, dust herself off and keep going. Nadia used this to rebuild her life, to make sure that her child would have everything they needed – a supportive mum, a roof over their head and unconditional love. Just 10 days after her baby was born, the UK went into the first COVID lockdown. Nadia's determination was unrelenting. Recovering from a C-section, she was having to carry a pram up two flights of stairs and as a single parent, recover and look after her newborn and their dog. She was getting barely 45 minutes of sleep a night and had no-one there to support her through those newborn days, and through the nightmare that COVID lockdown was. "It was actual hell on earth." But as Nadia has always done, she fought, she grafted, she endured it.

Nadia's relentless energy and creativity has never stopped. During those early years and lockdown, she experimented with starting new businesses. Four business ideas came and went before she settled on Kidfluence, an influencer marketing app. This allowed her the flexibility and stability she craved. After years of turbulence and turmoil, Nadia had finally found something that she loved, that was building, and that felt sustainable.

In late 2024, Nadia began to suspect she had ADHD. What followed was a journey of self-discovery, leaning into her past experiences, the good and the painful, and starting to make sense of patterns she'd never fully understood. Yet the path to formal support was far from straightforward.

Her GP repeatedly dismissed her concerns, refusing to process a referral as she wasn't 'ADHD enough'. It was disheartening and exhausting, but Nadia refused to give up. After months of persistence, she finally found a GP who listened, acknowledged her struggles, and supported her Right to Choose referral. She is now under ADHD360, currently progressing through the assessment pathway, a step that has already begun to bring clarity and validation after years of being denied it.

This realisation in October 2024 helped her to feel seen. She recognised that for years she had carried traits and quirks that others found strange or frustrating. Her hyperfocus could turn ideas into a reality overnight but the downside, she had a rejection sensitivity that left her feeling hopeless and worthless when her baby would push away food during weaning. She had masked for decades; she had learned to play a part, a caricature of who she really was on TV. The confident party girl, the life and soul, the version of herself that people wanted was just that, who she thought she had to be, who she had learned to 'play'. Unmasking has been hard, terrifying, but equally an enlightening process of rediscovery and acceptance for who she really is.

Nadia describes that, "Ignorance has been bliss in some ways. Knowing I have ADHD means I can finally be kind to myself". The realisation has been a blessing and a curse for her. She has talked openly about the journey of grief she has been on with this realisation. She is sad that she has lost many years of understanding of herself. She's spent huge parts of her past beating herself up for traits that weren't her fault. She wasn't lazy or weak, her brain was just wired differently. She is clear though that this knowledge has empowered her and opened the door to finding purpose and understanding herself.

Nadia's entrepreneurial success and the success of Kidfluence is not about the app itself. She is proud of the community she has created. She has built a space for founders to learn sales, marketing, and the mindset to be successful. The community shares the good, the bad and the real side of business.

Nadia doesn't romanticise about her journey; she is very honest about the highs and the lows. She also points to a pattern. "Everything I've ever wanted, I've worked hard, and I've eventually succeeded. How it looks is different, but it comes. I fail, I get up, I dust myself off and I move forward."

Reflecting on her childhood and who she is today, she shares that if she could go back and change anything, she wouldn't. "I wouldn't give myself advice, I wouldn't change my path. I would just give myself a long hug. A moment to feel safe and loved. That's what I needed."

The person Nadia is today, is a world away from the little girl who found herself just trying to survive. She's finding alignment and moving into the person she always wanted to be. She describes how she values soul contracts and how that forms everything she's doing and who she's becoming. Beyond the TV version of herself, beyond the mask, she is building something real, something to be proud of, both for herself and those around her. "I'm the best version of myself I've ever been. I know it's not about the destination, it's who I'm becoming on this journey."

Website: www.kidfluencegroup.com
Instagram: @ladynadiaessex
LinkedIn: @nadia-essex-45683841

Holly Matthews

Founder of The Happy Me Project® |
Award-winning Self-Development Coach | Speaker | Author |
Workplace Wellbeing Champion

Holly Matthews is one of those people who refuses to be put in a box. She's an actress turned singer, an author, an Intuitive Psychology Coach, and the Founder of The Happy Me Project. But to her daughters, she's simply 'weird, crazy, chaotic, funny, chatty, and silly'. Holly's life has been lived in colour, with all the chaos, courage, and creativity that ADHD so often brings.

Diagnosed at 35, it felt like a missing piece finally clicked into place. "For years, you just think you're disorganised, or chaotic, or that you've got to try harder," she says. "ADHD gave me an explanation, and a chance to reframe my story."

But Holly's story starts way before her diagnosis. She grew up in Newcastle-upon-Tyne with her parents and younger sister in a noisy, loving family that gave her the freedom to be her 'weirdest self'. Her dad worked on the oil rigs as a welder and later as head of health and safety in Kazakhstan, and her mum worked in banking. Her home life was warm, lively, and full of creativity. "I was described as a 'little hippie'." Holly recalls. "Always deep and reflective, always talking like an adult. My school reports said I struggled to connect with peers but loved talking to grown-ups."

"I was free to be my weirdest self. My sister and I spent our childhoods writing poetry and putting on plays." At 7 years old, she started drama classes at Newcastle's Live Theatre. The group was called Sit and Fidget. "That makes total sense now!" she laughs. "It was basically an ADHD club before I knew what ADHD was."

Her wider family also contributed to the lively atmosphere. "My dad and granddad were union men and had big personalities. My granddad, 'Matt the Cat', was well-known in Newcastle. In hindsight, I suspect he might have had ADHD." She lacked the language at the time, and so did others. "Growing up without the words, you just see yourself as different. You hide it. You develop ways to manage and blend in."

By the time she reached secondary school, Holly already knew she wanted to act. She began writing to TV shows asking for parts, undeterred by her age, or lack of connections. At 11, she blagged her age up to 12 and sent a letter in Comic Sans to Byker Grove. "That letter got me an audition," she says, "and eventually a part that turned into seven years on the show." That boldness, that willingness to 'just ask', became a defining feature of her life. "That impulsive energy has stayed with me my whole life. It's very ADHD."

Later, she would repeat the pattern. "I found Arianna Huffington's email online and thought, 'Why not?' I emailed her and she replied personally, not her team. She invited me to write for Huffington Post and Thrive Global. People ask, 'How did you get that?' Honestly? I just asked."

That impulsivity, sometimes reckless, sometimes brilliant, has been both a blessing and a challenge, but it shaped her path. Byker Grove opened bigger opportunities, and after leaving the show, she signed with Sony as a singer. "I never really wanted to be a singer," she admits. "I loved acting because it was a character, not me. As a singer, it was just me, and I felt exposed."

She released music, toured, did Top of the Pops, and MTV, but when her single charted at 32, Sony dropped her. "It was brutal, but the best thing that happened," she says. "It taught me resilience, to get back up and keep going." Drama school followed, then more TV roles in Doctors and Waterloo Road, plus modelling work. "I was always juggling multiple things, hustling between jobs, doing too much, typical ADHD energy."

Holly met her husband, Ross, on a modelling job neither of them were meant to be at. "It was instant," she smiles. "Love at first sight." He was funny, grounded, and sharp, with a directness that cut through the noise. Ross was autistic, diagnosed later, and likely ADHD too. "We balanced each other out," Holly says. "Where I was impulsive and all over the place, he had this calm, straight-to-the-point approach. He was my anchor."

Life was never simple. Both daughters had early health scares, and then Ross was diagnosed with brain cancer. "His approach was very direct: 'I'm dead or I'm alive. Why are we still talking about cancer?' That shaped everything. We handled it our way, not the way other people wanted us to."

Three and a half years later, Ross died. Holly was 32, a widowed mum with two young children, and suddenly her story was everywhere. "The press covered his death heavily. People came to my social media asking how I coped."

Out of that raw grief, and her need to make sense of life, The Happy Me Project was born. "It started as 21 self-development tips scribbled on the back of an envelope," she says.

Ross's death, and parenting her daughters through grief, brought ADHD into sharper focus. When her eldest went into therapy, the therapist suggested she might share some of 'Dad's traits'. For Holly, it was a moment of recognition. "That's when I started seeing myself, too. People had suggested I might have ADHD before, but I'd dismissed it. This time it clicked."

She pursued a diagnosis not only for herself, but because she had watched Ross face disbelief until his autism was formally recognised. "Being taken seriously matters," she says. "Without the right label, you get the wrong ones, lazy, dramatic, too much." Holly's ADHD diagnosis followed, and later medication. "It was life changing. Like having a highlighter for my brain. Without it, everything feels equally urgent. With it, I can focus. It's not perfect. It kills my appetite, private prescriptions are expensive, but it works."

Parenting her daughters has been both a joy and a battlefield. She recalls moments that still make her furious: "One of my eldest daughters' teachers, in an awareness lesson about Autism, drew a line on the board and said, 'This is the autistic spectrum. One end is really autistic; the other end is not. Where do you think you would be?' to a room of neurotypical kids. She was the only autistic child there."

Another teacher, frustrated by her eldest's Autistic quirks, casually told Holly she got it as she 'has OCD' because she liked things tidy. Holly pushed back: "When I was younger, I thought my family would die if I didn't touch every piece of wood. That's OCD. Being neat isn't." She's faced detentions for refusing to wear a polyester blazer "a sensory nightmare for her. She's immaculately dressed just without the blazer." Having multiple subject books has also been tricky for her daughter, but she found a system that worked. One neat notebook for all subjects, and the school banned it because 'Ofsted wouldn't approve'. "They punish kids for being different instead of celebrating when something works," Holly says. "If Ofsted came in, they should have been thrilled she was learning."

She has also had to advocate for her younger daughter. Whilst she is high-energy and empathetic, channelling everything into sport, because she is also calm and empathetic, she will often take on the role of 'carer', being the youngest child and because she lives with neurodivergent people. Holly is clear, though, that her daughter's age and right to simply be a child should be protected, especially in places like school, after-school activities etc.

For Holly, ADHD is a double-edged sword. Impulsivity and hyperfocus fuel her creativity, bravery, and instinct to press 'go'. But they also bring burnout, forgetfulness, and rejection sensitivity. Through Ross, her daughters, and her diagnosis, she's learned to own it, not hide it. "When I feel like I've upset someone, the intensity is ridiculous... it can feel like my world has collapsed. That's the side people don't see."

For anyone newly diagnosed with ADHD, juggling grief or starting out in business, Holly suggests: "Get to know yourself. Neutralise the shame. You're not broken; you just need scaffolding. Learn what helps you and ask for help with the bits you can't do alone. And lean into your weirdest self. Yes, you'll repel people, but you'll also attract the right ones. That's when things really start to happen."
To her younger self, she'd say: "Don't dim your light to make other people comfortable. Growing up on TV, making money when my peers didn't, feeling I had to make myself small, so others didn't feel put out, it made me underplay myself. I wish I'd believed earlier that it's okay to shine."

To her daughters, Holly is their weird, chaotic, funny, spray-painting doors so they can all have a 'dramatic exit', stylish, and hardworking mum, always putting them first.

To the world, she is unstoppable, embracing her ADHD, relentless and brilliant, fuelled by both pain and fierce positivity. Holly is unapologetic about who she is, showing what it means to lean into the weird, and live with courage, compassion, and fire.

Website: www.iamhollymatthews.com
LinkedIn: @iamhollymatthews
Instagram: @iamhollymatthews

Dodge Woodall

Festival Owner | Podcaster & Sports Promoter | Bournemouth 7s | Eventful Studios

The smell of hot dogs and ice cream still takes Dodge Woodall back to his childhood. At 10 years old, he was already running his own little empire outside his dad's London pub. "Every bank holiday, I'd set up an ice cream stand, and a hot dog stand. If it was sunny, I would sell loads of ice cream. If it was cloudy, I sold loads of hot dogs. I'd come out with £600 net profit as a 10, 11, and 12-year-old. I thought I was a multi-millionaire."

That hunger to create, to make things happen, never left him. Today, Dodge is the owner of Bournemouth Sevens Festival, the world's largest sport, and music festival of its kind. He's also the host of the chart-topping Eventful Lives Podcast, which has racked up more than 100 million views. An entrepreneur for over 30 years, he has built, scaled, and sold businesses, taken extraordinary risks, and more recently, discovered he has ADHD.

Dodge's childhood was unconventional. ""I lived in London as a kid in a two-bed flat above a pub, with a nightclub next door. My Mum and Dad ran the pub. I saw a lot of stuff kids shouldn't see, was always around adults, lots of laughter, lots of fun, lots of boozy people, lots of gangsters, lots of police raids. All wrapped up in one. Never to bed before 11 o'clock, seeing punch-ups, wheeling and dealing, fights, everything."

Amidst the chaos, he spotted an opportunity. By age 10, he was striking a deal with the nightclub manager next door, selling queue-jump tickets at a profit. He skip-dived at Toys R Us (behind the pub) for unsold toys to sell to parents outside the pub. He was relentless. "I was constantly earning money. And 30 years later, I'm still doing the same thing, selling tickets, only now to my own festival."

Academically, Dodge always felt out of place. Though he won a scholarship to a private sports school, his mind was never in the classroom. "I used to just stare outside. I wanted to be on the sports field, rugby, cricket, football, anything. Latin, algebra, chemistry, physics, I knew it wouldn't do me any good in later life. Maths, sport, and business were my things."

He became known as disruptive — not for causing trouble, but for asking questions. "I was always the one asking questions rather than answering them. Other kids would thank me for it. They were thinking the same thing. And today as an entrepreneur, if you're disruptive and curious, it's great."

Through rugby, Dodge found his way into Loughborough University. What he lacked in A Levels, he made up for with hustle. Deals with nightclubs soon meant he was making thousands in cash every week. "We hit the jackpot. From 2000 to 2008, I threw 1,500 club nights across the country. Then I moved out of nightclubs and created the Bournemouth Sevens Festival. No one had ever done a sports and music festival before. Eighteen years later, it's still going strong, 30,000 people in a field for three days."

Dodge's proudest achievement is also his riskiest. "Biggest achievement is gambling the family house and putting it on Bournemouth Sevens Festival in 2008 during the global financial crisis. It could have gone completely the other way. You're chucking in £300,000 on a party in a field and you don't know how many people will turn up, years before you bought tickets online. But 18 years later, we're still here, independently owned."

He adds, without hesitation, that the foundation of it all is his wife. "My biggest achievement is marrying my wife. You can't be a huge success without amazing support at home. If you've got someone who understands the late-night calls, the exhaustion, the holidays interrupted, that's everything."

Remarkably, Dodge only learned he had ADHD the night before our conversation. "John rang me and said, 'Dodge, I think you've got ADHD'. He arranged an assessment through ADHD 360 which happened the night before this interview which confirmed it. "I didn't even know what ADHD was. Didn't even know what it stood for. But after the assessment she confirmed, 'Yes, you're 100% ADHD'."

His reaction was characteristically upbeat. "ADHD? You could throw loads of letters at me, I don't care. I'm living a wicked life. It's worked for me. To me, it means I can talk about it on my podcast and socials and tell people: it's a superpower."

For Dodge, the gifts of ADHD are obvious. "If I love it, I'm obsessed. My energy is everything. If I'm around people who drain me, I'll just leave. I feed off energy and vibe."

He's also candid about the things he avoids. "I haven't opened a letter in 22 years. I haven't sent an email. I run everything off WhatsApp on my phone. I've built businesses without doing the stuff everyone else thinks is essential."

Friends know his restlessness well. "They call me Houdini. I'll just disappear from a restaurant or bar when I've had enough. I don't always say goodbye, I just leave." With age, he's found ways to channel it. "As I've matured, I've worked on myself. I'm direct, no fluff, straight answers. I love hearing brilliant ideas, and I get a buzz from them. I know what works, and what doesn't."

Dodge's drive is rooted in his family. His father, a well-known, respected person, gave him discipline. "Discipline is a beautiful gift, the willpower to say no, the discipline every day to keep going." His dad was hugely important to him as a child, and today. He describes him as his best friend, sounding board and the person he can tell everything. Dodge shares that "despite the craziness of living above a pub growing up, he gave me stability and so much love."

From his mother, Anne-Marie Woodall, came creativity, healing, and entrepreneurship. "I think maybe I pushed my mum away when they separated, because I was a dad's boy. But in her last two years, after she was diagnosed with cancer, we bonded. Those two years were the most beautiful thing of my life, because she knew she was going. She moved back and said, 'I've got so much to give you before I pass'."

Anne-Marie was a writer, speaker, and healer who travelled the world. Her book, Secrets of a High Heeled Healer, spoke about purpose, passion, and adventure. Dodge smiles at the memory: "She'd go on stage with a backpack and pull things out labelled love, happiness, romance, creativity, success, and vitality. She was a proper character."

He sees her traits in himself. "She had an amazing brain. She was so ADHD, now I look back. We were creating businesses together in her last year. That bond was special."

Dodge is clear about what matters. "Bad is when people are dying around you. Bad is horrible things happening. Business problems? I'm too resilient and have too much grit to worry about stuff that doesn't really matter."

He's equally clear on legacy. "We'll be dead in 30 years. After we're gone, no one remembers us after six months. You might as well leave a legacy. Leave something here so people can say, 'that was him', or 'that was you', 'that's what they did'."

And words matter. "Your word is your wand. Whatever words you use will happen. If you use negative, depressive, pessimistic words, that will happen. If you're optimistic and easy-going, things will fall into place."

When asked what he'd tell someone with ADHD at the start of their entrepreneurial journey, Dodge doesn't pause. "Start. Just start. Don't wait. Don't overthink. Get going. I recorded a solo podcast for the first time today. I thought it'd be weird, but I talked for 25 minutes straight. I realised I can do this. That's what people need to know, you can do it."

Looking back, his one regret is personal. "Maybe not to push my mum away. When my parents split, I took my dad's side. But I love mum to bits. We bonded later, and that was beautiful."

Dodge Woodall's life has been full of risk, relentlessness, and resilience. From selling queue-jump tickets at 10, to gambling his family home on a festival that would become a global institution, he has lived at full throttle, powered by self-belief, energy, and grit.

He refuses to see ADHD as a label that limits him. Instead, it is a key that explains his obsessions, his energy, and his need for fun, and connection. It is also the tool he now uses to lift others.

"I'm living a wicked life. It's worked for me. ADHD is a superpower. If I can tell people that, then maybe they'll start to see it too. And if they do, they'll realise they've got everything they need already, belief, energy, and the courage to start."

For Dodge, that courage has never been optional, it's the fuel that's carried him from the back room of a pub to the main stage of a festival, proving that with energy, grit, and relentless self-belief, you really can build the life you imagine.

Website:	dodgewoodall.com
LinkedIn:	@dodgewoodall
Instagram:	@dodge.woodall

Heston Blumenthal OBE

Michelin Star Chef | TV Personality | Food Writer

Heston Blumenthal is one of the most celebrated chefs in the world, but to describe him only in those terms would be to miss the heart of who he is. He is calm, humble, and endlessly curious, driven less by ambition than by emotion, and a need to question everything. Growing up, his mum would sometimes call him a 'stupid idiot'. Before he ever understood ADHD, those words and the way others responded to him began to shape how he saw himself and the world around him. What guided him wasn't a desire to be the best or to outdo anyone else, but a constant question: Does it have to be this way, or could it be done differently? That curiosity has shaped everything he has gone on to do.

He talks about his early life with honesty. School was never easy. His reports carried the same comments, 'must try harder', and whilst he enjoyed being there, he didn't excel. Exams and revision failed to capture his attention. He managed one A-level, in art, only because he stayed up the whole night before revising Hogarth, Reynolds, and Blake, and luckily for him, all three appeared on the paper.

The defining moment came not in a classroom, but on a family holiday in France when he was sixteen. His father, who had done well in business, drove the family south, and one evening they stopped at a restaurant. Heston remembers the scene vividly: the crunch of the gravel beneath his feet, the chorus of crickets, the intoxicating smell of lavender, the atmosphere of people eating together. It wasn't just about food. It was everything all at once and it's a moment of emotion, and sensory overload that stayed with him. He knew he wanted to become a chef, but he realised later that what he wanted was to recreate this multisensory experience for others.

Back home, he began buying French cookbooks, translating them word for word with a dictionary. Not long after, he found Harold McGee's 'On Food and Cooking', a book that explored the science of the kitchen, why rice behaves as it does, why eggs bind, why the reason for browning meat is a myth, and why soufflés rise. It gave him permission to challenge the rules he'd been taught. He didn't question them to be difficult. He questioned them because he wanted to know if there was another way, if something could be done differently, if something people had always accepted could, in fact, be 'not so'.

His day jobs at the time were ordinary: repossession work and bookkeeping for his father's business. None of it held his focus. What did, was cooking and kickboxing. He would take a single dish and make it twenty different ways. Every year, he saved money for months, and then spent it on escapes to France, eating lunch and dinner at as many restaurants as he could afford, and learning how they did the things they did. He built benchmarks in his head, the best soufflé, the sharpest ice cream, the most delicate pastry, and then went home and tried to replicate them. Always asking why.

That curiosity defined him. When McGee wrote that browning meat didn't 'seal in the juices', Heston's world shifted. Every chef he'd ever seen said it did. But in reality, meat contracts in the heat, squeezing out water. A well-done steak weighs far less because of it. It felt like realising something you'd been told all your life turned out to be a myth. It changed everything. From then on, he challenged every rule.

In 1995, aged 29, he bought a restaurant that would later become The Fat Duck in Bray. He and his ex-wife sold their cottage, he borrowed a little money from his father, and he moved back in with his parents. The building cost £240,000. Everyone told him it would fail. It only had one door, meaning staff, customers, deliveries, and rubbish all came through the same entrance. There was no parking. But he saw possibilities where others saw obstacles.

The early years were punishing. He worked 120-hour weeks, fuelled by adrenaline and determination and most likely, his ADHD and bipolar. He tried to light a blowtorch with hot water, fell asleep whilst filleting a fish, and once blew up an oven and burnt his scalp so badly that he directed his potwasher on how to serve dinner whilst standing with bags of frozen peas and chips pressed to his head. The menu began with simple French bistro classics, but within two years came crab ice cream, a first glimpse of the multi-sensory experiences he would later become known for.

Recognition didn't arrive overnight but gradually: a review here, a Michelin star, then another, then another. Eventually, The Fat Duck was named Best Restaurant in the World and now holds 3* Michelin stars. Television followed, but only when it added to his development, and to that of his restaurants. He insisted the food had to taste as good as it looked, because for him, it wasn't about spectacle. It was about emotion. He wanted people to feel something. He wanted them to leave with more than just the memory of eating; he wanted them to carry with them the wonder and connection he had first felt in France.

In 2017, more than two decades later, he was diagnosed with ADHD. A psychologist Heston knew suggested it, but he dismissed the idea. How could he have ADHD when he could focus for hours at a time? But that, of course, was the point. The restless brain, the hyperfocus, the forgetfulness, the scatter, the need to question everything. Suddenly it all made sense. The diagnosis didn't change who he was, but it explained the chaos he felt, and the brilliance he had achieved in equal measure.

He no longer describes himself simply as a chef, or even as a scientist, though both are true. He describes himself as being in the business of emotion. Food is his medium, but the end goal is something much bigger: to move people, to make them feel. Diners have cried at his dishes, overwhelmed by the emotions they evoke. For him, that is success.

Melanie, his wife, offers her own insight. She was diagnosed with ADHD the year after they met, and she sees him in words that are simple but telling: curious, passionate, and unconventionally creative. She says that with him, everything is done at 300%. Sometimes this shows up in funny ways, like the time he created a social connection and 'conversation' between talking toys, or when he simmered stocks for days on end, warning the cleaner not to touch the pot. Other times, it shows up in chaos: lost phones, phones in the fridge, random security checks at the airport with half-packed bags or random flamingos from home appearing in the case. But more than anything, she describes their life together as an adventure. "Nothing is impossible," she says.

She talks about how he doesn't give himself enough credit. When she first watched his old television programmes, she was struck by the sheer creativity and by the fact that he had built it all himself. For years, he couldn't accept compliments, moving on quickly to the next idea, but gradually, he has begun to acknowledge his own achievements. For her, his superpower is the way he joins dots, spotting connections nobody else would see, and turning them into something extraordinary.

Heston is clear about what he would say to someone newly diagnosed with ADHD who wanted to start a business. Find something you love, he says, and hold onto it. A diagnosis can explain so much and help you adapt. ADHD can make life chaotic, but if you have something that matters to you, it can become the focus that pulls everything else together.

If he could go back and speak to his younger self, aged ten or fifteen, he knows exactly what he would say: "Question everything." It is the thread that runs through his life. From the boy who never quite fit in at school, to the teenager who fell in love with food in France, to the man who blew up ovens, pushed himself to delirium and eventually built one of the most celebrated restaurants in the world, Heston Blumenthal has lived a life shaped by curiosity. It has been both his struggle and his gift. And for him, that is enough.

Website: www.hestonblumenthal.com
              thefatduck.co.uk
Instagram: @hestonblumenthalobe

Emma Walsh

Motorsport Presenter | Content Creator | Former Professional
Dancer, Singer and Stunt Performer

The roar of an engine. The lights of an arena. The quiet doubt before stepping on stage. For Emma Walsh, these are the markers of a life fuelled by adrenaline and performance, where every step forward meant breaking down stigmas and carving out space in areas that didn't exist for women like her, spaces she was told she didn't belong in, but claimed anyway.

Emma Walsh is a motorsport presenter, content creator, former professional dancer, singer, and stunt performer. Her career has spanned West End musicals, a girl band, YouTube stardom, and she has also worked across some of the biggest stages in motorsport. Her persistence is evident throughout her journey, she has the grit of someone who kept saying yes to opportunities, and knocking on closed doors, even when it terrified her.

Emma grew up in Somerset West near Cape Town, the daughter of English parents who had once been part of a well-known UK pop group, The Dooley's. She was always surrounded by music, energy, and the performing arts. "My Childhood was great. I was the middle child (middle child syndrome is a real thing, by the way), and I was just always left to get on with things. My parents being in a pop group is definitely where I got my performing interests from. I did well at school. I didn't like rules, but I didn't like getting into trouble either. After school, I was always in ballet, modern dance, piano, singing lessons. I just remember being busy all the time because I wanted to try everything."

Busy soon became the drumbeat of her life and by 15, she was working to save for her first car – constantly hustling to earn money. That determination took her to Johannesburg to dance and sing; she started an events company and later took to the seas performing on cruise ships. She worked as a backing dancer for some well-known artists such as Ja Rule, doing corporate gigs and eventually auditioned and secured a role in Grease the Musical. "We did a world tour, which then brought me to the UK in 2010 to audition for the West End Production of Grease the Musical."

The transition to life in the UK was brutal for her. "When I arrived, I had no backing, no money and so I started working hard to earn a living. I did every job I could: all promo work, handed out flyers at petrol stations, worked at events companies, a PA, dressed up as a Teletubby, and telesales. I then studied and got my PT qualification and taught classes at F45 and Kobox.

To leave my days free for auditions, I started doing extra evening work in night clubs as a waitress. Soon after, an opportunity to audition to be in a girl band on the X Factor came up. It was exciting and took her back into performing. It was her biggest achievement, and she felt like 'it was happening', but it was fleeting and would become her biggest heartbreak.

To this day, she still feels sad about this. It was hard for her as she felt like it should have been a moment in life that clicked. "Growing up in such a musical family, my parents being in a pop group, I always thought, one day that's going to be me. When I auditioned for the girl group and got in, I felt like, 'I've done this'. It was the brokest I'd ever been, but I was so happy. We had a huge contract, a big career ahead, psychologists, singing coaches, choreographers, a tour lined up. Then it all came crashing down. Biggest achievement to biggest heartbreak, almost overnight. Even now, I don't think I'm over it. I still feel like something's missing."

Beneath her outward success, a quieter reality was beginning to come into her life. "I always felt like I was struggling with things I couldn't explain. Misunderstood." As a middle child, Emma constantly felt like she was fighting for attention or approval. "It was a constant 'Hey, look at me, look what I've done'. When ADHD started trending on socials, I thought, 'That sounds familiar.' But then my inner RSD (even though I didn't know at the time that's what it was) would tell me 'People will think you're following a trend'."

It wasn't until listening to Alex Partridge's podcast and then through John Reynolds, being introduced to Dr Phil Anderton, that she finally sought an assessment. "The results were clear, I have ADHD. It's still fairly new, so I'm still processing. I'm learning about dopamine hits, figuring out medication. I've tried long release, but my day isn't the same every day. Now I'm trying a short release so I can manage better. I'm still figuring it all out."

The diagnosis unlocked more than just answers and validation; it has given her language to identify strengths she'd always had. "I'm deeply intuitive but can also doubt myself. I learn really quickly. Scripts, choreography, and interviews, I can pick things up fast. That helps me now. Also, when I have an idea, I'm like, 'I'm going to do this'. That keeps me knocking on doors (unless I procrastinate for a month!)."

But it also explained the struggles she had carried quietly. "Overwhelm, procrastination, doubting myself every day, rejection sensitivity. In performing, rejection was about the role, so I could excuse it. In social media, rejection was aimed at me. That was brutal. Even after a huge job, I'd come home and replay every conversation, beating myself up. Masking too. As a performer, I learned to be whoever I needed to be. It's helped me succeed, but it's exhausting. People think I'm outgoing, but I'm actually quite shy."

Her friends and colleagues notice her ADHD in small ways. "My flatmate says I switch tasks a lot. I'll half unpack the dishwasher, then remember the washing, then leave the fridge open. But I do always finish tasks. My manager knows and is a huge support; we're constantly finding new ways to work together. He understands me better, so we work around it. He'd probably say I ask too many questions, because I need to know everything, even if he's on it."

Backing herself has always been her way forward. "At racing events, I would often be the only female at events that were dominated by men. Being underestimated, particularly in these spaces, became a regular thing but that gave me more motivation to prove myself on the track."

If she could change one thing, it would be the rejection sensitivity. "That holds me back. I feel I could've achieved more without that voice in my head." And yet, there's a part she would never trade. "My ability to connect with people. It makes my interviews more authentic. I am such an empath though, and whilst it motivates me and that connection can be incredible, it does leave me depleted. I think I end up using all my energy, particularly at events, and then need a few days of quiet calm at home."

For others newly diagnosed, her advice is straightforward but heartfelt. "Talk about it. Don't be hard on yourself. Be patient. I wanted answers straight away, but it doesn't work like that. It takes time to find the right course of treatment for you, and you have to give yourself that time to really process it."

And if she could sit down with the girl she once was? "I would tell her she's not broken; her brain just works with a different instruction manual. One day, she'll get to read it and suddenly, it will all make sense. I would tell her she's not 'too much' and that her endless curiosity and questions are her superpower. In fact, one day, people will pay her to ask them! Oh, and don't listen to people telling you to choose one path. Eventually, people will call it being a multi-hyphenate (and it will sound really impressive on LinkedIn!)."

Emma's story isn't about a single stage, race, or broadcast. It's about carrying the grit of performance into new areas, taking risks when the script falls apart, and building her identity piece by piece. Her career is proof that you can do anything you set your mind to, if you have a passion for it; you can reinvent yourself, even when it means starting again at 32. What defines Emma is the courage and determination she has in continually showing up, knocking on those closed doors, saying yes to things that scare her, and forging the path that was meant for her, her way.

Instagram: @missemmawalsh

Afterword: Beyond the Book

Over dinner I was engaged in a fascinating conversation about ADHD and the music industry. There was a recognition that many people with ADHD have a significant creative flair, which, if discovered and unleashed, can lead to success in the arts.

As witnessed in his 'Beyond the Label' discussion, Marcus Beese OBE believes many, if not most, musicians he has worked with, an extensive list, have ADHD.

We then examined some of the elements of ADHD that are not listed in the mental health manuals and guidelines documents that clinicians rely on across the globe. In particular, a heightened sensitivity to rejection and significant struggles to regulate emotion.

When the conversation applied these impairments to the world of the Arts, particularly music, we identified a rather disturbing relationship between the Arts attracting neurodivergent people yet not understanding, maybe, the overriding and unique struggles that come with that, which appears to be a natural fit.

Musicians create new tracks, new approaches to the genre and do not always succeed. The struggle to find that 'hit' involves rejection; that popular track may get millions of Spotify downloads and the next track released may be a flop; rejections that need careful handling. A musician may not get a contract after all their hard work – another rejection. On the wave of success, the musician may be exposed to newfound wealth, exposure to alternative lifestyles, and may need to regulate their behaviour and emotions in ways never

315

witnessed previously. Knowing that we are correct that many in the Arts may be neurodivergent, could the industry do more? Could a higher level of understanding, an 'industrial' level of understanding, change the construct of how the music industry governs 'care' and makes accommodations? Staying with this example, could the industry therefore avoid the substance abuse, excessive and destructive behaviours associated with the artists that find, or do not find, success?

Far from a criticism of the industry under examination, this conversation should and will lead to 'next steps.' And once proven successful, could an industrial revolution of care in the Arts become a 'movement'? It should. Acting, art, performing in any guise, could we truly 'change the narrative'?

Dame Kelly Homes DBE was on a platform speaking at an event John and I were at recently and she boldly claimed, "No one jumps high if the bar is set low".

For many, the 'bar' in terms of understanding ADHD has been set and left far too low, for too long. Government Ministers are behind the curve in understanding. Most policymakers and leaders still don't truly understand what it means to be neurodivergent, aside from the few who are living it themselves. Teachers, meanwhile, receive little to no specific training in how to appropriately support neurodivergent children to actually learn.

What's needed is a fundamental shift in mindset: moving away from labelling children as having *learning difficulties* and instead recognising they face *difficulties learning* because the environments around them are not designed for their needs. That change alone could be transformative. The list goes on.

It is amazing to think that doctors and nurses are not specifically trained on how to recognise and manage ADHD in a clinical setting, and consequently, the link between undiagnosed and comorbid mental health diagnoses (either because of missed ADHD, or as a result of the impact of their ADHD) can be life-altering. The bar is set too low.

People with ADHD require a well-constructed, articulate, and passionate, yet objective voice so that we can raise the bar, remove the shame, and change the narrative.

This voice can, and perhaps should, come with the assistance of those in the media's eye that have persevered, made their luck, and worked through their neurodivergence to become a 'success', however that is defined.

This book is the start, or even a continuance, of that 'movement'.

Next steps include more of the same. A lot more. Through friendships and relationships, John, Frankie, and I hope to literally change the world for people with ADHD.

Together with you, the reader of this book, we hold and are lifting the bar to new heights.

The quest is very simple. In terms of a simple equation:

$$\text{Remove the shame} + \text{changing the narrative} = \text{a higher bar}$$
$$N - S = Hb$$

Phil Anderton PhD

Author, father, and stepfather to an amazing neurodivergent son, employer of many proud neurodivergent team members, and a man on a mission.

Acknowledgements

Without the honesty and emotion of the participants in this book it would be of little interest or value. To each of you, the team extend a heartfelt thank you. Your candour, and perhaps bravery, will change lives.

To the team that brought this to print against an impossible deadline, words cannot be enough. We hope that the pride you feel in reading this, and having the opportunity to discuss the content with others will give the intrinsic reward you so richly deserve.

To Natasha, for the hours of research, and interviews with everyone whose story appears in this book, her passion, tenacity and late nights to get the final draft finished.

To Kevin, for supporting the process, and organisation of the final hurdles.

To Linda, our editor, and Gary, at the Print Works, thank you for your hard work, and support making this book come alive and helping us to achieve our vision. It is more than a book.

To Tom Sullivan, our designer, despite the personal challenges that occurred at the 11th hour, delivered the stunning artwork. Great work as always Tom.

Our partners suffer and support in many ways, and I am sure they would say 'suffer – never!' with one of those knowing smiles, but we all know.

To the ADHD 360 community, the GBEA teams, the ADHD Beyond the Label production team, colleagues, and friends who enable growth for so many that need to see the narrative change, you are the best of the best. You hold a bar which, through the work you do, relentlessly day in and day out, gets higher and higher, allowing people to climb to new and exciting levels of achievement.

On a personal note, to my parents, looking down from the stars, I hope you are at peace and can finally look down on your firstborn with a sense of pride. You never got to witness any of my achievements, especially those that have led to success for other people. You are missed.

Phil Anderton, PhD

Final Thoughts

John Reynolds

Working with entrepreneurs is a stimulating environment to be in. The energy, the 'buzz', and the endless creativity are infectious. When the penny dropped that many of the people I work with have ADHD the understanding became tangible. It's my dream that this book helps us to change the narrative on ADHD.

Frankie James

It's incredible that we still don't fully understand ADHD. Whilst we have to focus on the symptoms and the impairment to have a diagnosis, come on guys, let's look for the positive. There's no shame in being different - and look at how that difference, as we've hopefully captured in this book, stimulates our economies and adds value to the world. It's an exciting set of optics on neurodiversity and one to cement change in thinking.

Phil Anderton

I've worked for over two decades with ADHD and I recognise that now, only now, we are on the cusp of change in how we appreciate neurodivergence in our communities. These are exciting times, and I hope our book motivates the reader to embrace being a little different, and to have the courage to move forward despite the challenges, emotions, and struggles that may lie ahead. Being part of a tribe and feeling that affinity is important - in fact, it's vital for wellbeing.